Canoeing In Kanuckia: Or, Haps And Mishaps Afloat And Ashore Of The Statesman, The Editor, The Artist, And The Scribbler...

Charles Ledyard Norton

Nabu Public Domain Reprints:

You are holding a reproduction of an original work published before 1923 that is in the public domain in the United States of America, and possibly other countries. You may freely copy and distribute this work as no entity (individual or corporate) has a copyright on the body of the work. This book may contain prior copyright references, and library stamps (as most of these works were scanned from library copies). These have been scanned and retained as part of the historical artifact.

This book may have occasional imperfections such as missing or blurred pages, poor pictures, errant marks, etc. that were either part of the original artifact, or were introduced by the scanning process. We believe this work is culturally important, and despite the imperfections, have elected to bring it back into print as part of our continuing commitment to the preservation of printed works worldwide. We appreciate your understanding of the imperfections in the preservation process, and hope you enjoy this valuable book.

By JOHN HABBERTON.

I. OTHER PEOPLE'S CHILDREN.
By the author of "Helen's Babies," . . $1 25

II. BUDGE AND TODDIE. An Illustrated Edition of "Other People's Children," 1 75

III. THE SCRIPTURE CLUB OF VALLEY REST; or, Sketches of Everybody's Neighbors, ... 1 00

IV. THE BARTON EXPERIMENT, . 1 00

G. P. PUTNAM'S SONS, Publishers,
New York.

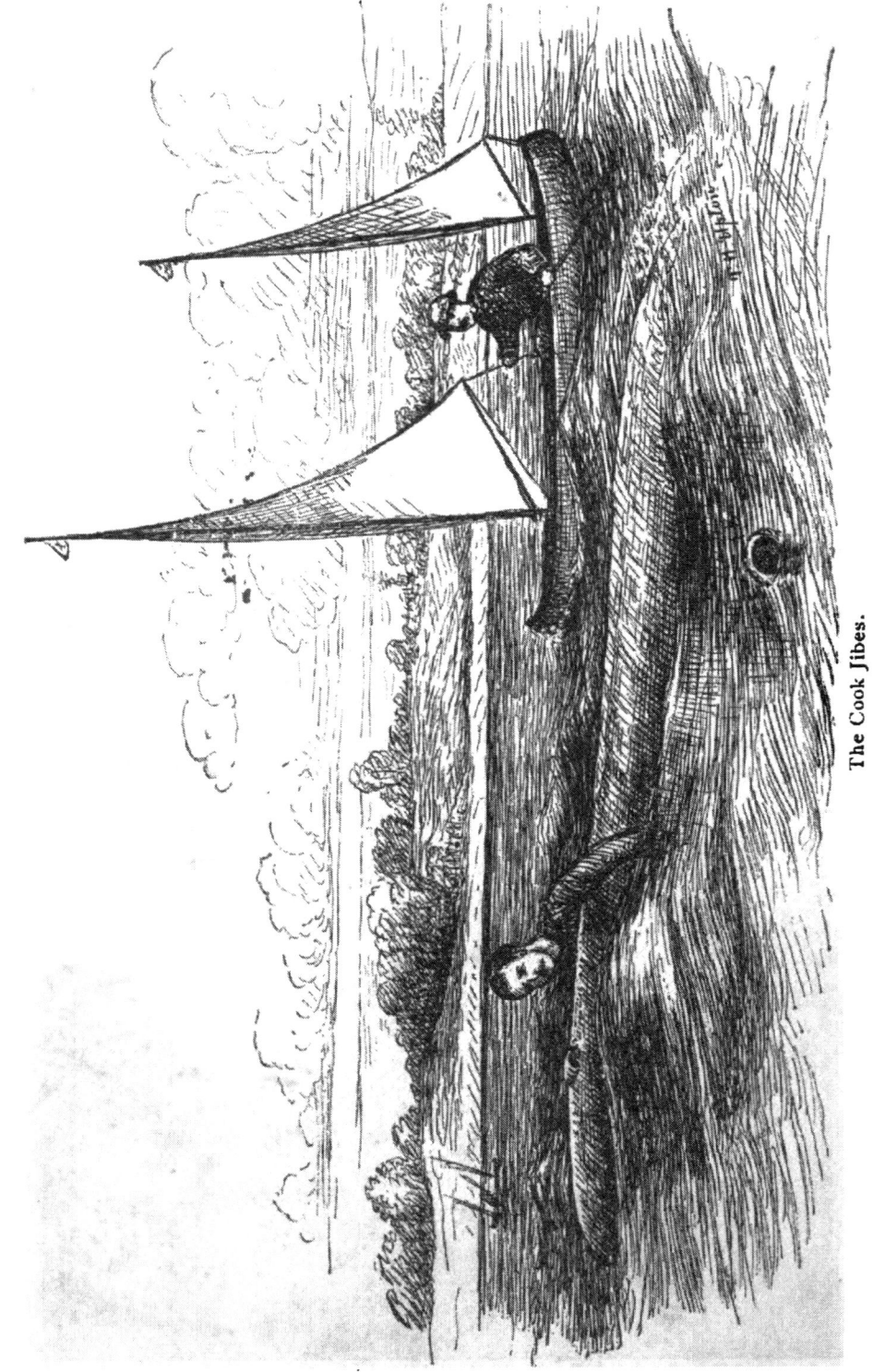

The Cook Jibes.

Canoeing in Kanuckia

OR

Haps and Mishaps

Afloat and Ashore

OF

The Statesman, The Editor, The Artist, and The Scribbler

RECORDED BY

The Commodore and the Cook

(C. L. NORTON AND JOHN HABBERTON)

ILLUSTRATED

NEW YORK
G. P. PUTNAM'S SONS
182 FIFTH AVENUE
1878.

Copyright by G. P. Putnam's Sons, 1873.

DEDICATION.

THIS

VOLUME

IS

AFFECTIONATELY INSCRIBED TO THE MEMORY OF

KING CANUTE,

WHO TOOK

A

ROYAL DUCKING

WITH AN EQUANIMITY WHICH FAIRLY ENTITLES
HIM TO RECOGNITION

BY

THE CANOE CLUB.

PREFACE.

MELANCHOLY as the admission must necessarily be to persons with aspirations toward literary Art, the authors are forced to acknowledge that most of the incidents recounted therein actually occurred during a canoeing cruise to the Northward, in which they were participants; that the localities described have a geographical existence, and that the persons introduced and the experiences recorded are, with trifling exceptions, true to the life. They frankly admit that they might not have been so truthful had they suffered from lack of incident, but their perplexities have arisen from too much good material instead of too little. Departures from strict veracity have been made solely on the ground of good fellowship.

The authors being blessed with ordinary human perception, it is not strange that they fully realize their own superiority to their companions in point of virtue, manliness, good-seamanship, personal appearance, adaptability, etc., etc. They have thought it simply honorable, therefore, to separate individual traits and experiences, each by themselves, and redistribute them without prejudice or partiality among the entire quartette.

As the ~~effect of this generosity~~ has been to cause some doubt on the part of each member of the expedition as to his own personal identity, it is certain that no one of them can be successfully reconstructed by any outsider. How unalloyed a blessing the public thus enjoys, is not for the self-renouncing authors to point out in detail.

P. S. BY THE COOK. It has been found impracticable to prevent the Commodore from causing to be inserted in the following pages certain efforts of his own which he is pleased to denominate "Sketches." He is apparently actuated by the hope that they will pass for professional work. The real Artist of the expedition, however, being solicitous regarding his own reputation, wishes it distinctly understood that he is responsible only for those illustrations which are signed by him in full, and has deputed the Cook to warn the public to this effect.

CONTENTS.

	PAGE
INTRODUCTION	15

I.
GETTING UNDER WAY 21

II.
COOKS AND COFFEE POTS AND SEAMANSHIP 38

III.
THE COOK STUDIES NAVIGATION 49

IV.
THE WRECK OF THE ROCHEFORT 68

V.
SUNSHINE AND SHADOW 80

VI.
MY NATIVE LAND FAREWELL 88

VII.
GARRISON LIFE 111

VIII.
THE BEGINNING OF ACADIA 129

CONTENTS.

IX.
AREAS OF RAIN 145

X.
ACADIA 166

XI.
SEVERAL OTHER DAYS 181

XII.
A CHANGE OF SCENE 206

XIII.
SWIFT WATER 212

XIV.
MORE RAPIDS 223

XV.
THE BEGINNING OF THE END 229

APPENDIX 249

LIST OF ILLUSTRATIONS.

		PAGE
1.	The Cook Jibes	2
2.	The Authors	20
3.	Mlle. Rochefort at home	22
4.	Chrysalis and Chrysalid	23
5.	The Twins	24
6.	Kayak Birch, Rob Roy	26
7.	Under full sail—Chrysalid	28
8.	Close hauled. Red Laker	30
9.	The Quartette	32
10.	The local Small-boy	33
11.	Coffee Pot before	43
12.	Coffee Pot after	44
13.	A Sporhungan	46
14.	The Sanctuary	48
15.	The Cook selects a Boom	50
16.	Gosh	57
17.	The Vice's Boom toggle	58
18.	The Commodore's Sprit	59
19.	Island Camp	61
20.	A Vigorous Pull	63
21.	A little too vigorous	65
22.	Aquatic Leap frog	66
23.	"His ship she was a wrack"	69
24.	The Cook's Tent	78
25.	Green grow the rushes	83
26.	"But the Consul's brow was sad"	89
27.	The United States Garrison	93
28.	The Purser on British Soil	94
29.	A Canoe Seat	99

ILLUSTRATIONS.

		PAGE
30.	The Picturesque afar	101
31.	The Picturesque anear	103
32.	Wahu ei	104
33.	Supper Table	107
34.	An unknown Fortress	112
35.	The British Garrison	115
36.	The Sally Port	116
37.	The Vampire Bat	118
38.	The Commandant	120
39.	The Commandant's Lady	122
40.	The Dock	133
41.	Under the Elms	139
42.	The Enchantress	142
43.	Boat, Aristocratic	146
44.	Boat, Plebeian	146
45.	The Commodore Weather-bound	147
46.	Aux Armes Citoyennes	153
47.	Alone with his Conscience	159
48.	The Typical Church	161
49.	Water Front	168
50.	Down the Rapids	170
51.	No Ruins in America (Ruskin)	174
52.	Canadian Loaf, etc.	171
53.	A Quiet Cove	177
54.	A Charming Landscape	186
55.	A shock to the Commodore's Nerves	188
56.	Use Laundry Soap and be Happy	205
57.	Down the Race	210
58.	In the Second Rapids	208
59.	The Vice sits for his Portrait	218
60.	Comparative Coffee Cups	226

INTRODUCTORY.

"GO see her?—certainly I will!" said the Artist.
"So will I!" exclaimed the Scribbler, jumping to his feet and rearranging his neck-tie; "if she is half as beautiful as you say, I'd go every day to see her, even were the trip twice the score of miles that it is."

"And I," said the Editor, replacing in his vest-pocket the folding-scissors which he nervously fingered by force of professional habit.

"'Tis done, then," said the Statesman, "she will be at my house to-morrow evening and the winter through, but she is particularly handsome and graceful just now, and there's no time like the present, you know. Dine with me to-morrow evening: I'll give you a tip-top spread, but when you see *her* you'll forget it all."

"We will come!" shouted the Artist, the Scribbler and the Editor in chorus, and when twenty-four hours later the trio fulfilled their promise, they admitted that the half had not been told them. They exhibited however, none of that unseemly jealousy which would naturally be expected from a trio of admirers at sight of an almost phenomenal beauty, for the object of their admiration was a canoe, and accepted their attentions with an impartiality which would have been the envy of any society queen. She occupied the study of the Statesman, and covered almost as much space as if she were a lady with a train of the first magnitude; she was in every line the embodiment of grace, and her beauty was not entirely independent of paint and other cosmetics. But here the parallel ceased. In visiting a canoe the visitor enjoys certain liberties which are not admissible during an ordinary evening call. A gentleman may speak in most enthusiastic praise of a canoe, and right to her face, without being suspected of a desire to flirt; he may criticise freely without seeming unmannerly; he may even talk admiringly of other canoes without disturbing the outward or inward complacency of his fair entertainer. He may even unlock his wits with a good cigar without provoking a cough from the fair being, and without compelling her to send her finer adornments to the bleachery next day, or expose them on the family clothes-line, to the purifying breezes of heaven. One may look fixedly by the hour at a beautiful canoe without being guilty of ungentlemanly staring, and may thus call up all those finer sentiments which far transcend the powers of expression, and may thus elevate his own nature to a degree which is unattainable under the restrictions of a fashionable call. He may without offence or even discourtesy, touch her, though if he be a man of true character he can not do so without a struggle with natural timidity, and without a new sense of his own awkwardness.

The quartette gazed, and smoked, until the fair outline before them became veiled in the soft haze which so enhances the glories of a perfect form and a rich complexion. They talked, they mused, they talked again; the Artist, the Scribbler and the Editor talked of their own special darlings of the same genus. They mused again, then they fell once more to admiring. The one blot upon the perfection of the being before them was that her sole guardian had christened her "Rochefort," but the Statesman, like statesmen in general, had his weaknesses, and if men cannot be tenderly enduring of the weaknesses of their friends, what statesman can live? At length the Rochefort's protector broke silence by saying,

"Can you fellows gaze upon her, and talk of her rivals, and then refuse to go on a cruise this summer?"

"Not I!" exclaimed the Editor.

"Refuse?" exclaimed the Scribbler, and then he betrayed his Hibernian ancestry by adding, "I'd go alone, for the sake of having her with me."

"And I know just where to go," said the Artist. "I know of a picturesque lake whose outlet is a placid river flowing through an Acadia like that which Longfellow has pictured, and breaking at last into wild rapids down which we can run like salmon in the fall."

"Is Evangeline still there?" asked the Statesman, with symptoms of lively interest.

"She is every where," replied the Artist.

"Why," said the Statesman, examining his mental memoranda, "she died two centuries ago."

"She is perennial," answered the Artist, and the Statesman inwardly cursed his own literal perceptives.

"Let's take our sentiment when we are there," suggested the Editor; "this is the hour for action."

The conversation which ensued need not be detailed here. It would consume so much ink and paper as materially to raise the price of these staples. It is sufficient to say that the quartette silenced forever the calumnious statement that only ladies talk two or three at a time, and that the necessary supplies decided upon for the trip exceeded in bulk the cargo of that most capacious vessel, the Mayflower.

The Authors.

CANOEING IN KANUCKIA.

GETTING UNDER WAY.

ALL night the Statesman, the Editor, the Artist and the Scribbler had been rumbling northward in a sleeping car, and as day dawned the steady and quickened clank of wheels told that they were on a down grade toward the Lake, and nearing the point where vacation was really to begin. They had turned into their respective berths somewhere south of Albany; they awoke and looked down from a precipitous hillside into the clear Lake. Presently the train slowed and in another minute they were questioning the station-master about their canoes, which had preceded them as freight some days before.

"No, can't wait till after breakfast. Must see them now."

So the station-master rather reluctantly unlocked his freight room and there in a row side by side lay the "Red Lakers" and the "Chrysalids," for all the world like two pairs of twins tucked in a big bed together. For the station-master—bless him!—had thoughtfully spread a

Mlle. Rochefort at home.

tarpaulin over them so that only their darling noses were in sight.

It should here be explained that the terms " Red Lake " and Chrysalid " designate certain models of canoes, the first being named for the locality where the canoes are built, while the appropriateness of the second must be evident from the accompanying sketch.

Let the *Expeditionis Personæ* now be introduced.

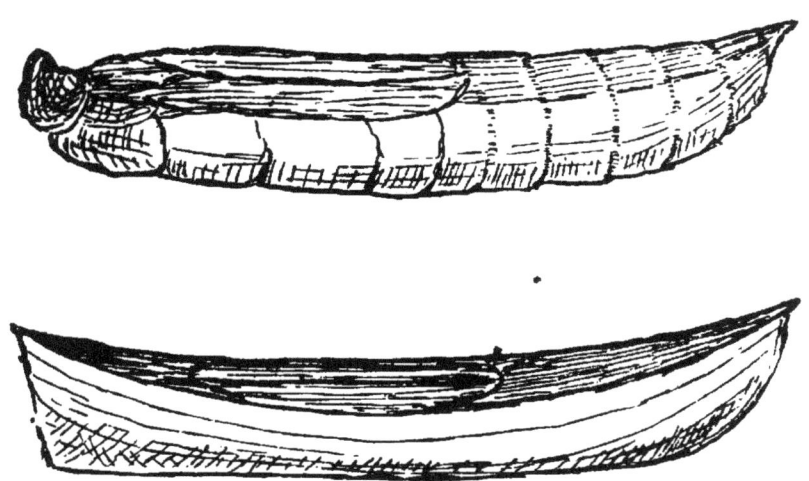

Chrysalis and Chrysalid.

Behold the BECKY SHARP (flag-ship) and the CHERUB, commanded respectively by the Editor and the Scribbler, and constituting the "First Division." Behold also the " ROCHEFORT " and the " ARETHUSELA "* forming

* The artist begs the authors to explain that this name is the result of a compromise between the friends of two domestic cats "Arabella" and "Methusela," neither of whom would consent to have the boat named exclusively after the other.

The Twins.

the Second Division, and commanded by the Statesman and the Artist.

Over the meeting between each man and his canoe a veil is delicately drawn. Even the station-master considerately stepped out upon the platform during the few moments when each metaphorically made his canoe put out its tongue and answer questions as to its moral and physical well-being. The interview was satisfactory to all save the Statesman, who detected several minute scratches on the deck of the Rochefort and declared that palpable demoralization had resulted from her enforced association with Red Lakers.

The Artist having volunteered to stay by the boats while his companions breakfasted at the neighboring tavern, was straightway beset by a number of wayfarers who demanded full accounts of the canoes and of canoeing in general. The Artist had been in the lecture field, and as the spirit was strong upon him, he gave the assembled multitude (about a dozen in all) a comprehensive account of the art. No reporter was present, but his remarks are believed to have been about as follows:

"In the civilized acceptation of the term, gentlemen," (here the six small boys who composed a fraction of the audience punched one another in the ribs,) modern canoeing dates back only a few years,—some fifteen in England and half as many in America. Its acknowledged progenitor is Mr. John Macgregor, an English barrister to whom was vouchsafed the brilliant idea of crossing the canoe of the North American Indian with the Esquimaux Kayak, for purposes of civilized recreation, the product being a hybrid known as the Rob Roy model. (Here the speaker seized the station-master's chalk and drew rapidly upon the wall in illustration of his meaning.) Although the

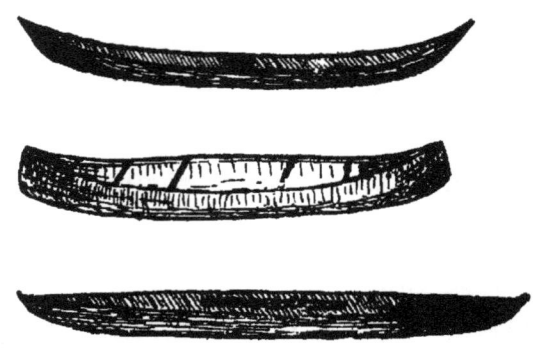

Kayak—Birch—Rob-Roy.

canoe exists among all savage nations, it reached its greatest perfection for inland and coastwise navigation among the North American Indians. The 'birch,' as it is familiarly called, is so nearly perfect for use on forest streams that the Hudson's Bay Company, after various experiments with wood and iron, settled down, years ago, to its almost exclusive use for their vast transportation service extending throughout the British American Possessions. The Kayak, built as it is of a light frame with skin stretched over it, has less weight and more strength than the birch, and as it is all covered over excepting a man-hole amidships, it is evidently the more seaworthy of the two. It has, however, no carrying capacity to speak of, beyond its crew of one."

"A different craft from either of these is required for the use of the civilized voyager. He wants a boat which will not, like the birch, leak if it happens to touch bottom. He wants one which will retain its buoyancy even when full of water; which at a pinch he can carry alone across a portage; which is roomy enough to sleep in, large enough to carry stores and equipments for a reasonable number of days, staunch and seaworthy in any weather when it is pleasant to be on the water, and readily obedient to his hand under sail or paddle.

"No doubt Mr. Macgregor drew his first inspiration from the two barbarian models referred to. He designed a boat known as the 'Rob-Roy,' which was easy to paddle, which could be slept in, and in which he made many long cruises. It was, however, decidedly faulty in many particulars, being wet and uncomfortable in a sea-way, owing to its lack of 'sheer;' it was also of small sailing capacity. In smooth water, the 'Rob-Roy' has its advantages, but for general purposes the 'Nautilus' model is decidedly its superior. This was designed by Mr. Baden Powell, another Englishman, who improved on Mr. Macgregor's model by giving his boat greater 'bearings,' that is, a broader and flatter bottom, that of the original Rob Roy being nearly semi-circular, and by raising her lines at stem and stern so that it was nearly impossible to drive her nose under in a sea-way. This made her very difficult to manage under paddle with the wind abeam, so in subsequent plans the sheer was considerably

Under Full Sail—Chrysalid.

reduced, and the change proved to be a decided improvement.

"The 'Chrysalids' (here the speaker indicated the Arethusela and the Rochefort) are variations of the Nautilus type. You perceive at a glance their great superiority in every particular over the 'Red Laker' (pointing to the Cherub and the Becky Sharp) which lie beside them, and which are merely elaborate copies of the Indian birch made of wood and rigged for cruising. I will draw for you a Chrysalid under sail." (The Artist turned again to his extemporized black-board and with a few rapid strokes produced the sketch on page 28.

Meanwhile the local population had dropped in one by one, until he had a respectable audience, and the Scribbler, who had finished his breakfast and drawn near, began to consider the expediency of taking up a collection.

"You see how ship-shape she is in all respects, (applause, the Artist bowing,) I will now, in order that my fellow voyagers may not accuse me of partiality, show you also a Red Laker under sail." Again the station-master's chalk was in requisition, and presently a sketch something like this adorned the wall. As the Artist was proceeding, a youth near the door, who, the Artist vows, had been bribed by the Scribbler, checked him with, "I say, mister, that there Red Laker makes the best looking picter of the two, don't it?"

The Artist had not compared his illustrations, and on

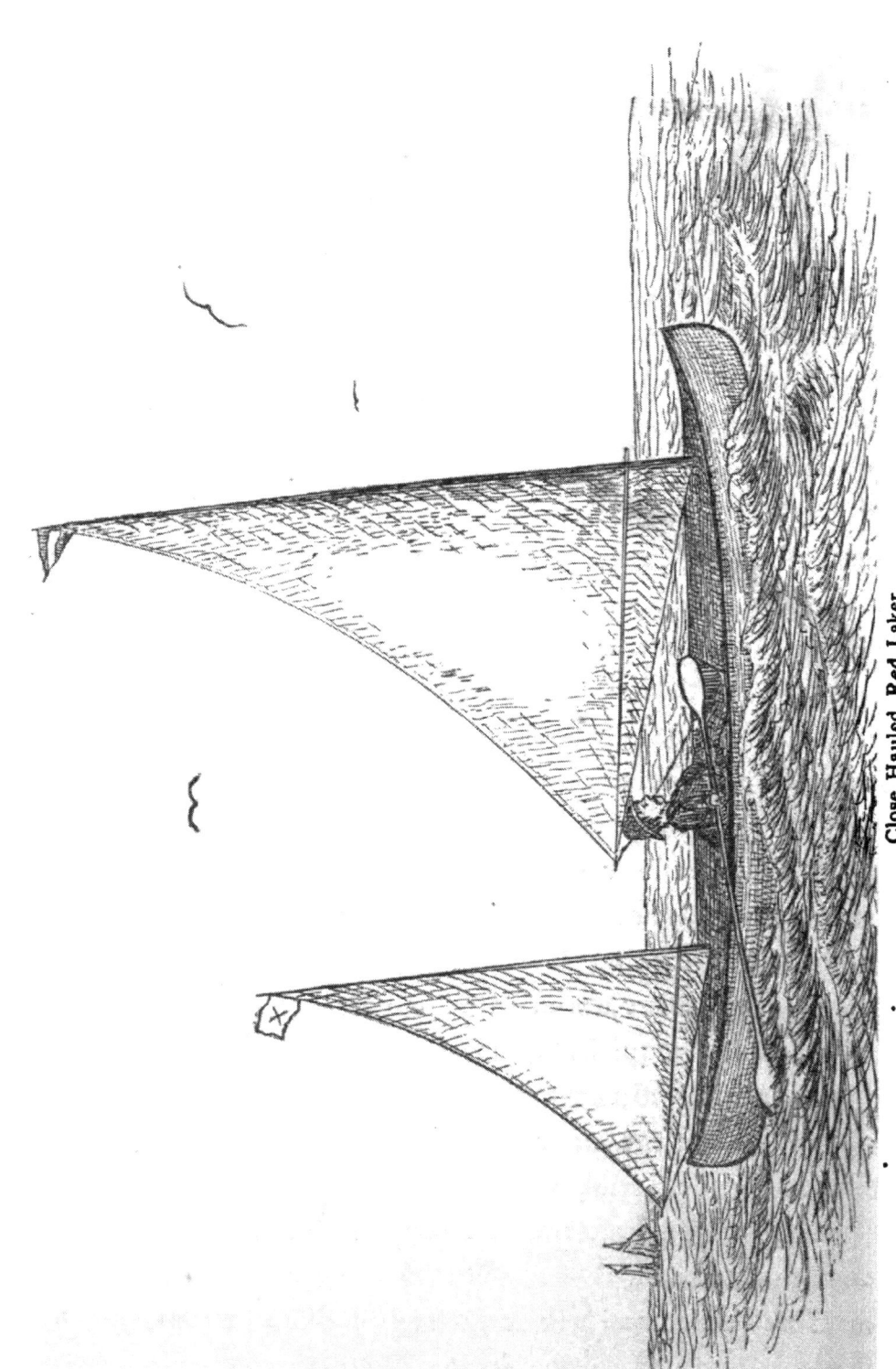

Close Hauled Red Laker.

glancing at them, was obliged to explain that certain peculiarities of outline assuredly did give a false impression in this instance :—However," he went on easily, resuming the imperturbable manner which had become habitual with him in the desk, "as I was about to say, having thus become Anglicized, it was merely a question of time how soon the modern and improved canoe should be re-naturalized in America. It was introduced in 1872 by Mr. W. L. Alden, founder and senior member of the New York Canoe Club, an association to which the boats before you belong, and which now has a fleet of about thirty canoes, and a somewhat larger number of active and honorary members."

The Artist ceased and the Scribbler led off in a round of applause, which was however, but feebly seconded.

Breakfast over, the quartette donned their blue flannels and sauntered down to the shore, followed by a curious throng of the inhabitants. (N. B. The throng of inhabitants is seen at the right.)

The Lake, which at an early hour had been placid as a anglican sermon, was, by the time the fleet was ready to start, breaking furiously against the wharf before a northerly breeze and the mariners were glad to launch and stow their canoes under the lee of the railway bridge, and the critical supervision of the local small-boy.

For six months the four comrades had made preparations for the cruise, but the knowledge which worketh experience worked also calamity, for the stores which

The Quartette.

were unloaded from steamboats and express cars on the shore of the lake, would have justified each captain of a canoe in chartering a steamer of moderate dimensions as

The Local Small Boy.

a tender. As such a course would have tended to the destruction of the picturesqueness of the squadron under sail, it was given up without a murmur, so the quartette, each man for himself, proceeded to the exasperating duty of deciding what he best could spare and return. The Statesman decided against carrying a tent, a tin pail, a couple of hundred weight of canned goods, a life-preserver, a Bible and a looking-glass which he had brought with him, but retained a double-barrelled gun, a twenty-pound bag of duck-shot and a volume of Tupper's "Proverbial Philosophy."

"If your boat springs a leak, no earthly power can save her, with such a cargo," said the Editor.

"I'll keep the shot where I can drop it overboard in such case," briskly replied the Statesman.

"What good will that do?" asked the Editor, "if the Tupper remains on board?"

"The Tupper will make a capital anchor, though," suggested the Artist, as he reluctantly laid upon a heap, to be returned, a field easel, a camp-stool, a medicine-chest, a set of Shakespeare in three volumes, and a demijohn, the latter, by some deplorable oversight, having arrived empty. The Scribbler carefully inspected two bulky portmanteaus, extracted therefrom a single change of underclothing, a box of cigars, a tooth-brush and a comb, and returned the bags with their contents. The Editor concluded that perhaps he might be safe in Acadia without the copy of Webster's Dictionary which he had brought thus far in several thicknesses of rubber cloth, and a mental survey of the proposed route convinced him that he might dispense with his faithful scissors and paste-pot, inasmuch as no newspaper was published on either the Lake or the River, but he stowed in his boat a gold headed-cane and a horse-pistol, explaining, as he did so,

"These are the interviewer's only faithful friends."

The individual property thus rejected, with the superfluous stores which had been purchased *en bloc* by the quartette, threatened for a little while to cause a "corner" in freight cars, but a threat to charter several steamers which were idle upon the Lake brought the railway agent to his senses, and gave his Company an excuse to put upon Wall Street a story of sudden increase of gross earnings. The rejected cargoes were stowed, and then the Editor, calling his companions apart from the immense crowd of gazers and listeners, said,

"Gentlemen, by virtue of long experience as a fighting editor, I hereby assume command of this expedition, and propose to be obeyed and respected accordingly. I detail the Statesman as Vice-commodore, commanding the Second Division."

"Vice," murmured the Artist, "what an ideal title for a Statesman!"

The Commodore continued, "The Artist I appoint Purser—"

"What delicious sarcasm!" interrupted the newly appointed Vice; "the idea of an Artist taking care of money! Judas and his bag are nowhere."

"And the Scribbler," resumed the Commodore, "will be Cook, a position to which his experience in concocting literary hash most richly entitles him. During the cruise all family, baptismal and social names will be dropped, and the members of the expedition will be known only by their nautical titles. Is every one ready to embark?"

"Ready!" replied the Vice, the Purser and the Cook in chorus; the paddles were seized, and the Commodore was giving the command "Shove off!" when the Vice exclaimed,

"Gracious! how could I have forgotten it?" Then he ran to the pile of rejected material and rescued an immense brown paper parcel containing something which seemed to be instinct with every angle and line known to the student of conic sections. Hurriedly stowing it away in his forward compartment, he shoved his boat from the beach.

"What is it?" shouted the fleet.

"It was a present to me from a constituent," roared he, at the top of his lungs, the wind whisking away his words. "That's what it is."

This was accepted as a diplomatic and statesmanlike way of saying "None of your business," so the rest held their peace, and gave themselves to the serious work of making headway against the sea.

'Tis ever thus! Never have any of the Four started on a cruise without having at the very beginning to tax their as yet unaccustomed muscles by paddling straight in the teeth of an adverse gale. Of course the canoes are at their heaviest and must be expected to leak more or less after a fortnight's baking in a box-car. So when all are ready the command paddles round through the draw, points toward a headland three miles off dead to windward, and doggedly settles down to its work. It takes nearly two hours to cover the distance, and the Chrysalids have had to bail at frequent intervals under the protecting care of Red Lakers. The headland is reached at last, however, and then comes the bath for which all have been longing. If any future explorer finds an unaccountable deposit of cinders and scoriæ off that point he may ascribe them, if he likes, to prehistoric volcanic convulsions, but the four voyagers know better.

It was now noon, and a substantial luncheon was followed by a long siesta under the cedars, while lungs accustomed to inhale the de-oxidized atmosphere of the city filled themselves with the first draughts of ozone from the great paradise of spruce which stretches almost unbroken from the Canada line to the Arctic circle. Grand mountain forms rose against the sky, the city was far away; they were free!

The sun lacked but three hours of setting, when the squadron shook off the delicious languor that succeeded its unwonted exertions, bailed out the Chrysalids, now thoroughly soaked, and in a condition which their owners were pleased to consider "tight," wiped up with a sponge the few drops that had penetrated the seams of the Red Lakers, and paddled merrily away toward an island blue in the afternoon haze, on which it had been determined to camp over Sunday. The lake was by this time ashamed of the boisterous welcome it had given to the fleet, and was undergoing a burnishing process preparatory to serving as a mirror for the sunset. By dusk camp was made in a lean-to left by some considerate predecessors. The canoes were anchored in the lee of a shingly point, excepting the Rochefort, which her commander carefully, and for some inscrutable parliamentary reason, anchored to windward, and by nine o'clock all, with one exception, were rolled in their blankets, and sound asleep.

II.

COOKS AND COFFEE POTS AND SEAMANSHIP.

AS is the case in all well regulated families, the Cook was the first person to greet the morning of the second day. He not only did so, but he greeted it in its extreme infancy, an instant after his own watch, had it been a repeater, would have struck midnight, and from this moment onward he manifested the liveliest interest in the growth of the new day. His impatience could scarcely be attributable to a desire to see the sun rise, for at home the Cook habitually rose at dawn, and had already an unequalled collection of sunrises in his mental portfolio. In truth, the Cook was very cold. He had smiled pityingly as he saw his companions retire each under a pair of woolen blankets, while he himself stretched freely upon his rubber sheet, with no covering whatever. Woolen blankets in July, when at midday the thermometer stood at ninety degrees in the shade!—the Cook perspired anew at the thought, and chuckled over the superior good luck which had led him to forget his blankets when he left New York, thereby materially reducing the bulk of his equipment. Woolen blankets might be necessary to the city existence of the Statesman, the Editor

THE COOK'S PREDICAMENT.

and the Artist, for each of the gentlemen represented professions which are notoriously cold-blooded, but as for the Scribbler—well, all scribblers come early in life to regard blankets as rarely attainable luxuries, and to depend for warmth upon their own inner man.

But on this particular occasion the inner man of the Cook failed to respond to the demand made upon it. The Cook would have encouraged the inner man had he known where the expeditionary brandy was kept, but no racking of memory elicited the information desired. He scraped carefully among the ashes of his evening fire, hoping that some coals might have remained alive to kindle a new one, but the fire had been of wood too small to leave coals, and the Cook's matches were wet. He might have had dry matches, brandy—yes, and a share in the blankets themselves, all in an instant, had he but awakened either of his brother officers. But the Cook's pride exceeded in greatness even his discomfort, so he sought consolation in his own reflections, as men are always possessed to do at just such times, when their reflections are in the most shocking condition imaginable. The Cook paced the sand, hugged himself, and tried to believe that there had been no such day as yesterday, and that he had never left a blanket in New York. Then he tried to draw his rubber blanket noiselessly from the tent, to throw over his shoulders, but one side of the Purser rested upon its extreme edge, and the Purser was of the conventional English ponderosity. Then the Cook tried to revive his spirits with a song, sung softly between his teeth, but these last named gateways of sound were trembling so that the song itself became sadly demoralized. The Cook had once written a convincing essay on "The Power of the Imagination, as Exemplified by Physical Facts," and recalling this, he soliloquized "Physician, heal thyself!" Honestly he endeavored to obey the injunction, by imagining himself burrowing in a whole bale of Mackinaw blankets, as he had once done in the far west when smitten by an ague, but the warmth was as imperceptible in the former case as in the latter.

The night wore on, to the extent of two or three thousand hours, and reduced the chilling Cook at last to a single desire:—he wished that before he froze to death he might have a thermometer, a pencil and paper, and record for the benefit of coming canoeists this terrible temperature.—if, indeed, the thermometer could indicate it before the mercury itself would freeze.

Then came that mysterious hour of the night in which night, itself still regnant, trembles at the prospect of its own dissolution. It was the hour in which sick men who are foredoomed to die generally accept the inevitable: it was also the hour in which the Commodore, in his home capacity of Editor, always left the office of the "Daily Tocsin," and walked home with a sedative cigar for company. The force of habit being strong in the Commodore, he rustled uneasily under his blankets, and finally emerged from the tent, filling a pipe as he came.

"Just the man!" exclaimed the Cook. "*I* want to smoke, but I hadn't the heart to awake any one to beg a dry match."

Both pipes lighted, the Cook remarked,

"D–d–don't you think it would be more cheerful to smoke by a f–f–fire?"

And the Commodore, with a very perceptible flavor of irony in his tones, replied,

"I d–d–dont know but I d–d–do."

Five minutes sufficed in which to make a roaring fire: then the Cook scraped up a ridge of sand a few feet from the blaze, allowed it to heat, stretched himself against it and was asleep in an instant. An experienced seaman, however, when in a position of grave responsibility, never allows himself entire freedom from care. Hence in the present instance the sailor-like instincts acquired by the Commodore during long years of sedentary life, caused him some anxiety as he once more lay down in the tent. The wind had freshened from the southward, and he deemed it his duty to arouse the Vice whose canoe, as has been stated, was anchored off a lee shore while the rest were securely sheltered behind a point. The reply elicited by his appeal was somnolent rather than respectful, and the Commodore resolving upon disciplinary measures in the morning, once more arose and sought the beach. Professional instinct had not been at fault. There was the Rochefort full of water, rolling heavily in the trough of the sea, and banging her cedar broadside against the stony shore. With that devotion to the service characteristic of the true sailor, the commanding officer laid aside at once his trowsers and the dignity of his station, and rescued, at the risk of wetting his remaining garment, the vessel which the inexperience of a subordinate had imperiled. In this connection it may be well to remark that a stone which weighs twelve pounds out of the water weighs only about seven beneath its surface. Ignorance of this simple mechanical principle led a well-meaning and occasionally meritorious officer into the error of using such a stone for an anchor.

Still the Cook slept when the Commodore returned from his labor of love, and crept shiveringly into his blankets.

The hours passed, the sun arose and beat upon the Cook's face, and still he slept. By the time the occupants of the tent awoke the sun had performed his toilet so thoroughly that not a dewdrop remained visible. But still the Cook slept, and when the Vice saw him he took in the situation at a glance, and remarked:

"Methinks I remember a cruise in which the Alderman was temporarily without blankets."

The Vice performed his ablutions, shaved himself, eyed the fire, walked impatiently around the Cook, and finally exclaimed:

"Boys, I'm starving, but it's too bad to rouse that tired wretch. I'll take his place this morning. He does well enough as a cook, but he has some silly notions that

THE VICE'S COFFEE POT.

I'd like to reason him out of. He always cooks with hot coals; now I propose to show him that a bright blaze is just as useful, and far sooner made ready. Besides I am

The Vice's Coffee Pot before.

the proud owner of a utensil which is destined to revolutionize the art of coffee-making." The others were fain to acquiesce in this arrangement, but the Purser, with characteristic prudence, put some water to boil in the regular way. The Statesman meanwhile burrowed among his stores and shortly appeared bearing the brown paper parcel which had excited curiosity at the beginning of the voyage. Tearing off the paper he exhibited a structure of the general appearance depicted.

"Here," said he, rapidly resolving it into its component parts, "is the receptacle for the coffee. And you fill this part—no, this one—with water. Then you put it on the fire. As soon as it boils you turn it bottom up. Let's see—no, it was bottom up before; you turn it right ade up and there you are. Coffee strained, not boiled." This last with a contemptuous glance at the sleeping cook.

The Vice piled wood upon the fire, and while it blazed up fiercely he hastily filled the wonderful coffee-pot half full of water, and set it in the midst of the flames. Five minutes later the Cook awoke from a dream of hearing a tin peddler's wagon upset on a stone pavement. Rubbing his eyes he beheld the Vice, with a long hooked stick,

The Vice's Coffee Pot after.

rescuing various pieces of tin from the fire, and dropping them upon a boulder near by.* The flame had resolved the wonderful coffee-pot into its dozen or more original fragments, and as the Vice made a final dive for the spoutless, handleless, topless vessel, the Cook drawled:

"Some people cook over coals, and some prefer a blaze."

"Why," spluttered the Vice, as he blew upon a burned

* In order to protect themselves against prosecution for libel the authors would state that the coffee-pot in question is an admirable one under proper conditions. Such conditions, however, are not afforded by an open fire of drift-wood.

finger, "the Alderman always made coffee over a blaze."

"Then he did it in a coffee-pot with a bail which hooked on, instead of being fastened by solder. And besides he suspended it over the fire after this fashion."

The Vice walked away to his boat in disgust, while the rest seated themselves about the unprofessional breakfast which had been made ready. Presently he sauntered boldly among them with what he was pleased to term a coffee-cup in hand, looking rather red in the face, but sturdily demanding his breakfast.

"Some of that potted salmon, Purser. Pass us the bread, Commodore. I say, Cook, isn't that coffee ready yet? Commodore, this thing won't work. If fellows are going to shirk their share of the drudgery, the service will go to the dogs. What I want is my coffee, and I want it NOW, do you hear, Cook?"

But the Cook was magnanimous, for he had a coffee-pot of his own, and though the Vice contended that the coffee made therein had not the aroma peculiar to that made in the one which he had loved, and lost, he revealed the hollowness of his plea, (or his stomach) by drinking twice as much as any one else did.

The Flag officer deemed the moment a fitting one to administer, firmly but kindly, a merited rebuke to the subordinate whose heedlessness had on the preceding night imperilled the safety of a valuable vessel. On being asked if he had anything to say in his own defence, the disgraced officer replied with unblushing effrontery that he was warm and comfortable when the Commodore waked him; he was sleepy, and he knew the Commodore would

A Sporhungan.

get up and do what had to be done anyhow, and he didn't want to get up in the cold and—

Here the Commodore broke in with an authoritative "Silence, Sir," but as the rest of the fleet went off in convulsions of irreverent laughter, he thought it best to let the matter drop.

Saturday is a good day to begin a canoe-cruise. The unwonted exercise induces weariness which the first night in camp does not wholly remove, so that a day of rest and a second night of more refreshing sleep, are usually acceptable to all. Opposite is what the voyagers looked at from their camp, throughout that peaceful Sunday.

At this camp too, the regular details were permanently

IN POSITION.

and formally arranged. The Scribbler having confirmed the Commodore's judgment, and evinced a decided genius for cookery, consented to serve permanently as *chef*, the rest taking turns on successive days as foragers, wood-cutters, and dish-washers.

The Sanctuary.

III.

THE COOK STUDIES NAVIGATION.

AS the squadron turned out and took its matutinal swim, soon after sunrise, the lake was dimpled by a favorable breeze, and after breakfast orders were issued to make sail.

"I've got to make a spar first, Commodore," exclaimed the Cook, "my main boom is gone, or hasn't come, I don't know which."

"Find another at once," said the commanding officer, and the Cook seized the hatchet, and started into the timber, returning presently with an elm pole weighing twenty pounds, nearly half the weight of his boat, his original boom having been a piece of bamboo weighing a scant half-pound. By dint of hard work with hatchet and knife, he worked this log into a makeshift for a boom.

"I wonder," remarked the Cook, as he dropped his knife for a moment, and caressed the blistered palms of his hands, "why all you fellows insist on having decks. I don't wonder that you two Chrysalids," referring to the Vice and the Purser, whose boats were of that famous model, "I don't wonder that you two Chrysalids do it, for the builder of your boats stupidly decked them before you bought them, but the Commodore, who, like me, was sensible enough to buy a Red Lake boat, wasn't satisfied to leave it free and open as he found it, but has gone and

The Cook selects a Boom. (Below is the one that was lost.)

stretched rubber-cloth over it fore and aft. It's as bad as sailing in a coffin, to sail in any of them."

"I'd as lieve sail in a coffin as in a bath-tub," replied the Vice, who, having commanded a blockade-runner during the late unpleasantness, had a natural fondness for tight decks and plenty of them.

"A well-covered bath-tub," remarked the Commodore, "is fully as sea-worthy as a mahogany topped coffin, and far less suggestive of canoeing on the Styx. But for a cover of some sort, I confess an affection. It keeps things dry; if a man capsizes—"

"A canoeist has no business to capsize," interrupted the Cook, who had learned canoeing on a Western river, and in a "dug out," which could only be turned over by the united efforts of at least two men, "and a canoeist has no right to have 'things' lying so loosely as to drop out."

At length the squadron set sail. The wind had freshened, and the white caps were as numerous and agitated as in a large female seminary during a night alarm of fire. The Commodore, the Vice and the Purser were all experienced sailors, so they shortened sail, but the Cook, having never handled a boat under sail before, possessed his soul of the nautical bliss that comes of ignorance. Shorten sail? He would show those fellows what a fearless sailor and a good boat could do, when the wind was disposed to aid them. The Cook experimented nervously for a few moments to learn where the sail should really be to catch the most wind, but when he learned he made full use of his knowledge, and his boat, the Cherub, seemed literally to fly. It passed the Becky Sharp, (the flag-ship) so rapidly that the Cook had not time to study the Commodore's face long enough to know how that official liked it; it passed the Rochefort, causing the Vice to scowl as if the unoffending Cherub were a member of the party which the whilom statesman hated; it threw for an instant the shadow of its great white mainsail on the Arethusela, darkening the blonde complexion and golden locks of the Artist-Purser.

Then the Cook began to enjoy his boat and himself.

A pistol which he had in his pocket to be ready for a shot at some passing water-bird, chafed him somewhat, and he laid it in the bottom of the boat, where it would be equally handy and less troublesome. He had heard that a canoeist should always be barefooted, so he kicked off his shoes. He pitied his comrades who sat upon the hard bottoms of their boats as they sailed, while he sat upon the many folds of a large tent. All the inner lines of his beautiful canoe were before his eye, instead of being hidden by decks, as those of his companions were—if, indeed, there were any beautiful lines any where about their boats.

The Cook was happy; he fastened the sheet of his mainsail to a cleat, softly whistling, as he did so, "A Life on the Ocean Wave," neither thinking nor caring that the ocean was really several hundred miles away. He was astonished and delighted that sailing was so easy an art to acquire, but pshaw—sailors, like poets, are born, not made. Had not one of his ancestors sailed with Drake when that hero interfered with the sailing directions that had been delivered to the Spanish Armada? What might he not have achieved himself, had cruel fate not ordained that ink should be his only fluid element? Just here the Cherub made such astonishing speed that the Cook determined roughly to "time" his boat, so he estimated a mile of distance by the trees upon the shore, opened his watch and laid it in the bottom of the boat, before his eyes.

But Solomon said that pride must have a fall, and when there is any unpleasant saying of Scripture to be fulfilled, a conceited canoeist is as good as any one else that can be selected for the purpose. The squadron was approaching a point beyond which its course would be changed. The Commodore shouted "Ready about!" and the Cook's self-confidence disappeared as rapidly as if it had been the conscience of a congressman after an interview with a "subsidy" lobbyist. "Jibe!" shouted the Commodore. The Cook, almost in despair, looked astern, to see what the others did. He saw their masts straighten, their sails flap irresolutely for a moment, and then fill on the opposite side. How was it done? Accident came to the Cook's rescue: a wretched steersman at best, he had almost forgotten his helm as he looked astern, and an unintentional turn of the wrist of his steering hand turned the boat's head from the wind. Around came the new boom; the Cook had never before seen a boom come around on his own boat, and he had no idea of how close the same would come to the plane occupied by his own head. But the time occupied by an industrious boom in jibing is not sufficient for prolonged meditation, and while the Cook was wondering what to do, the boom attended faithfully to its own business. The elasticity of a green elm log is an unknown quantity; the Cook's dome of thought was equally inelastic, so the Cook soon heard a heavy thud, as when one throws a mighty stone at a well-laden chestnut tree. Then the Cook heard a splash, and he was not allowed to remain in doubt as to the object which caused it. All the terrible stories he had heard about men who had been carried down by the sails and rigging of capsizing boats came hurrying into his mind, and he swam so vigorously to escape a similar fate, that his boat had time to turn leisurely over and adjust itself to its new condition before he dared to pause in his mad career. (*See Frontispiece.*)

Then the Cook swam to his boat, and resting an elbow upon her keel, gazed pensively around him. Something that seemed to be a peculiarly-shaped dark fish, a little way below the surface in front of him, proved to be the slowly sinking form of one of his shoes, going to join its mate. A black bundle, consisting of most of the Cook's personal effects wrapped in a rubber-blanket, was rescued by the Commodore just as it seemed discouraged by the difficulty it experienced in floating. The Cook's hat, one of the paddles, a covered tin pail containing butter, a worthless bit or two of board, and sundry other articles of little value, were picked up by other members of the expedition, but the indisposition of watches, pistols, and even wet tents to wander aimlessly about on the bosom of a lake is known to all students of comparative specific gravities. The Cook groped for the painter of his own boat; his other hand he rested upon the stern of the flagship, and thus the demoralized couple reached the shore. The remainder of the squadron had already disembarked, and the Purser made haste to extend the hospitalities of a private flask, but he robbed the draught of its flavor by asking, as he passed it,

"Shall I explain to you why canoes are usually decked?"

And the Cook was so absorbed in contemplation of his bare feet, that he did not even look up. At length he inquired as to the depth of the lake; the Vice obligingly paddled to the scene of the disaster, took soundings, and reported fifty feet. To go through fifty feet of water to cover two feet not over dry was not to be thought of, but what hope was there of replacing lost shoes in a wilderness—even when Acadia was reached, the natives probably made and wore only wooden sabots.

The overturned boat was righted, and the Cook emptied his portmonnaie and laid his money on a sheltered rock to dry, while he should change his clothing and restore his boat. Then the Commodore, consulting a chart, discovered that there was a village only ten miles distant on the border of the lake, and it was large enough to justify a hope of shoes: the squadron should put in there. The delighted Cook proposed an immediate start, particularly as a force of small boys was approaching. The village was reached, the Cook found a pair of shoes, but on attempting to pay for them he remembered having left his money on a stone to dry. And that stone was ten miles away, it could only be reached by paddling against a head wind, and when last seen the ground containing the stone was occupied in force by boys! The

Cook, as he walked back to his boat, was in a savage frame of mind, and wanted to hurt somebody or something, but no one would laugh at him, or offer sympathy Suddenly his eye fell upon the extempore boom; a moment later and that faithful spar which had done only its honest duty, sank deeply in the lake. The Cook's credit was good, however, and he succeeded in borrowing from the Statesman enough money to pay for the shoes and a blanket, and buy a bamboo fishing-pole from a casual youth who angled on the adjacent wharf. This was speedily converted into a boom of proper size and weight.

"The rest of us may as well go booming, too," remarked the Commodore, who had been strongly stimulated by the exhibition of spirit in which the Cook had indulged. By this time there had gathered about the squadron quite a crowd. It was, however, a crowd of great conservatism; each man seemed to have in his pocket a valuable something, which required the unremitting contact of his hands, as well as something in his mouth which would escape were he to part his lips. Occasionally, however, one would release a hand long enough to test the weight of the Vice's canoe, which was the only one that had been drawn entirely out of the water, and as each of the sixty odd men present did this at least once, gravely uttering, as he did so, the monosyllable "Gosh!" the Vice was extremely delighted. The expletive recalled the days of his innocent youth.

Gosh.

"It is plain to see," said he, "that living right on the edge of monarchical institutions as they do, these poor fellows have never before seen a boat of any lightness and grace."

"Don't forget, please," remarked the Cook, "that my canoe, which is lighter and faster than yours, was made in Canada."

Having repaired damages, the squadron proceeded, paddling side by side along the shore in search of favorable camping ground.

"How does the Alderman toggle his boom, Vice?" asked the Purser, who during the day had his own private

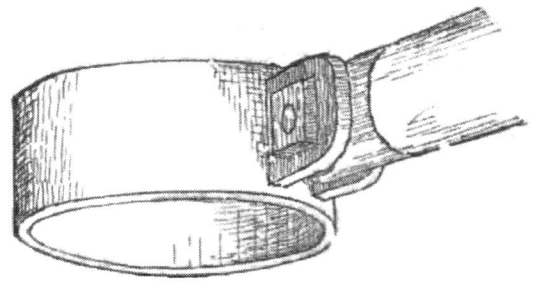

The Vice's Boom Toggle.

troubles with that important spar, and was beginning to have some misgivings as to rig.

"Same as I do mine, with a brass collar for the mast, and a screw and bolt arrangement to make the boom fast. See?" And the Vice exhibited his boom where it was attached to the mast.

"That's just like mine," said the Purser, "and I don't altogether like it. I believe simple jaws and lashing, such as you see on any sail-boat, are more convenient."

"No true canoeist will sacrifice style, merely for convenience," replied the Vice sententiously. "Now, there is more style about a Chrysalid than about a Red Laker, and that more than compensates for their inferior speed, and carrying capacity, and so on. Every man should have his boom rigged in the most complicated manner. Now

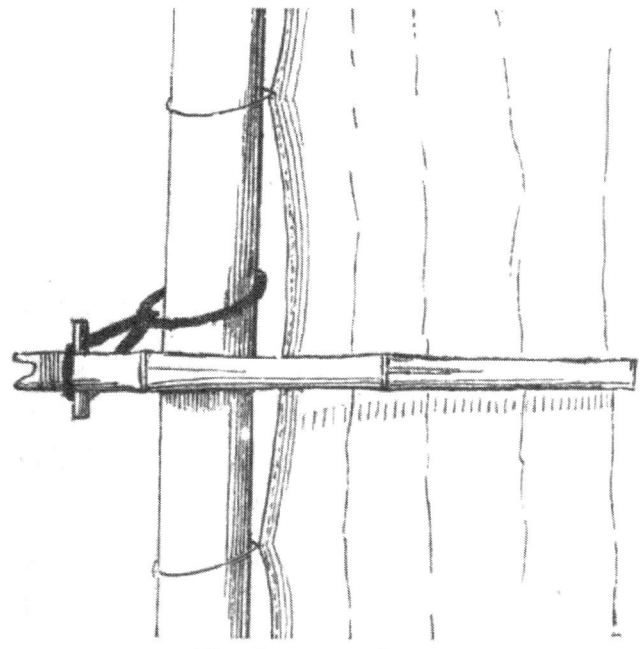

The Commodore's Sprit.

look at the Cook, and the Commodore. See their booms, (The Commodore accommodatingly held up the foot of his mast for inspection,) or sprits rather. They are not properly booms. Now, that rubber band passed through a ring, and over a cross-head or a notch on the end of the sprit, undoubtedly keeps a light sail flatter than any other contrivance I know of, but there's nothing ship-shape about it. 'Twouldn't be allowed for a moment in the navy. You want something that it takes some skill to manage."

"Thanks," said the Purser, "I see the thing in its true light now," and he went to work when camp was reached and fitted jaws to his boom, and even threatened to adopt the leg-of-mutton sprit-sail before he went cruising again.

"I don't see," commented the Cook, "why the india-rubber arrangement should not be adapted to a boom as well as a sprit. It only requires a little ingenuity, and would keep the sail quite as flat as does your present rig."

Rounding a promontory the fleet sighted a wooded island three-quarters of a mile from shore, and as such an island is for several reasons preferable to the main land for camping, they made for it at once and found it all that their fancy had painted. The fleet with one exception was hauled upon the beach, but the Vice, anxious to retrieve his reputation for seamanship, made fast the painter of the Rochefort to a stone which he could hardly lift and hove her short under the lee of the point. The flag-officer silently noticed these preparations, but said nothing, resolved not to interfere again between the Rochefort and her commander.

Here again it was found that former generations of campers-out had sojourned, leaving their lean-to, scientifically constructed of poles and bark, standing for the accommodation of posterity. As the sun sank black bass

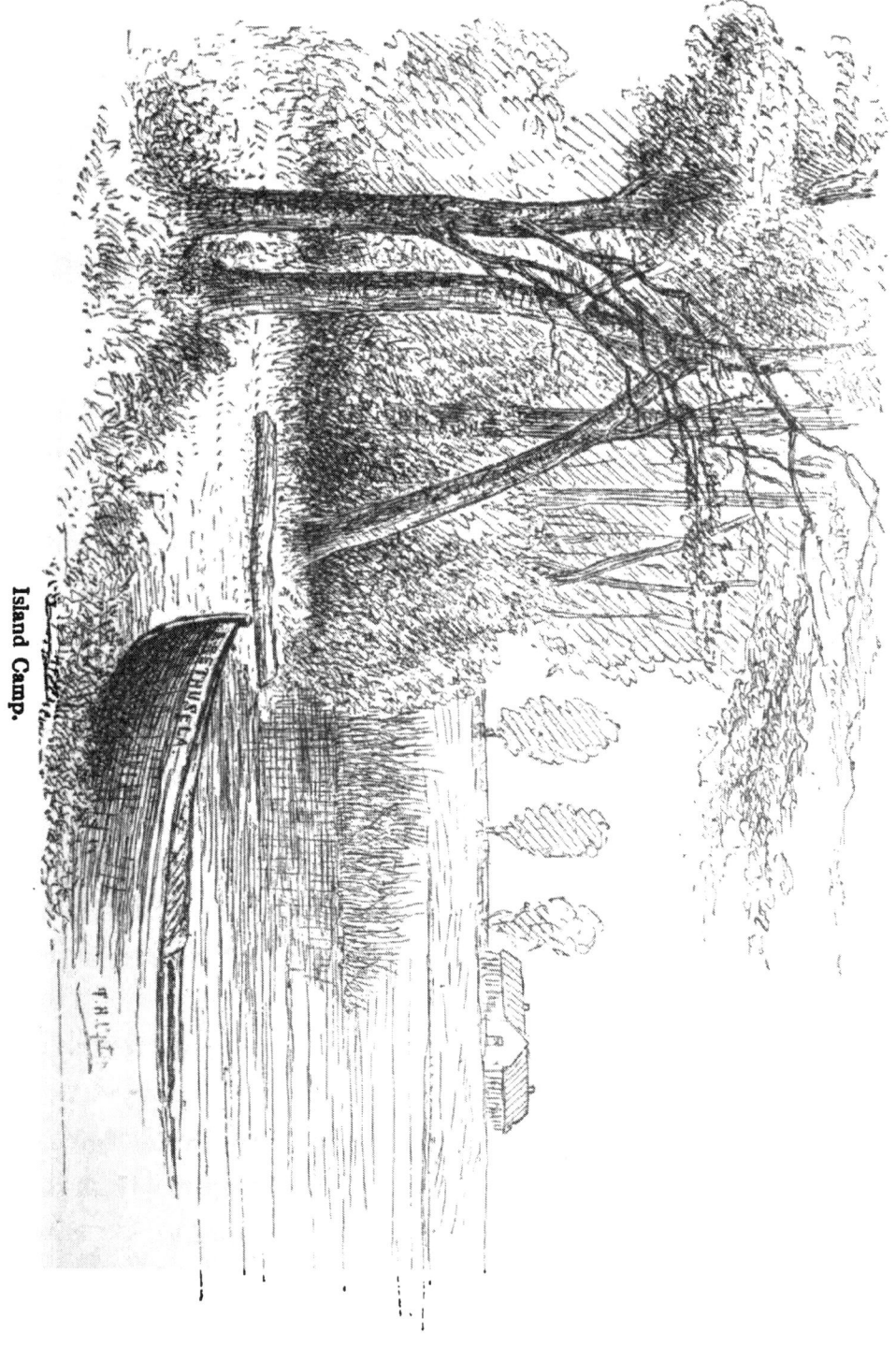

Island Camp.

began to break the glassy surface of the lake in search of their evening meal.

"Would that the Alderman were here," remarked the Vice, as he watched the circles widen on the water, and heard the inspiring splash as the fish flashed up in the sun's rays, "he would catch us a string of bass and show the cook how to fry them, in less than half an hour."

But the Commodore had been putting his rod together, and having in the course of the day killed a large bull-frog, he now lashed a portion of its hind leg to a hook with fine thread and quietly launching the flag-ship, stood up in her amidships and made a cast as far out toward the feeding ground as possible. A vigorous pull rewarded his effort and almost as soon as the Alderman could have done it he had two thumping bass and a good sized chub, or dace, which the Purser and Vice cleaned and the Cook fried to a turn for supper.

"The Alderman would not have stood up in his boat to catch these fish," said the Vice with a crisp "second cut from the tail" on his plate, "that kind of thing isn't regular."

"No; it would be decidedly irregular in some boats," remarked the Cook.

"I'll bet you cigars for the crowd—my choice ones, that I've preserved carefully in my water-tight,—that I can throw a line from a Chrysalid."

"Done."

The Arethusela had nothing aboard, so the Vice bor-

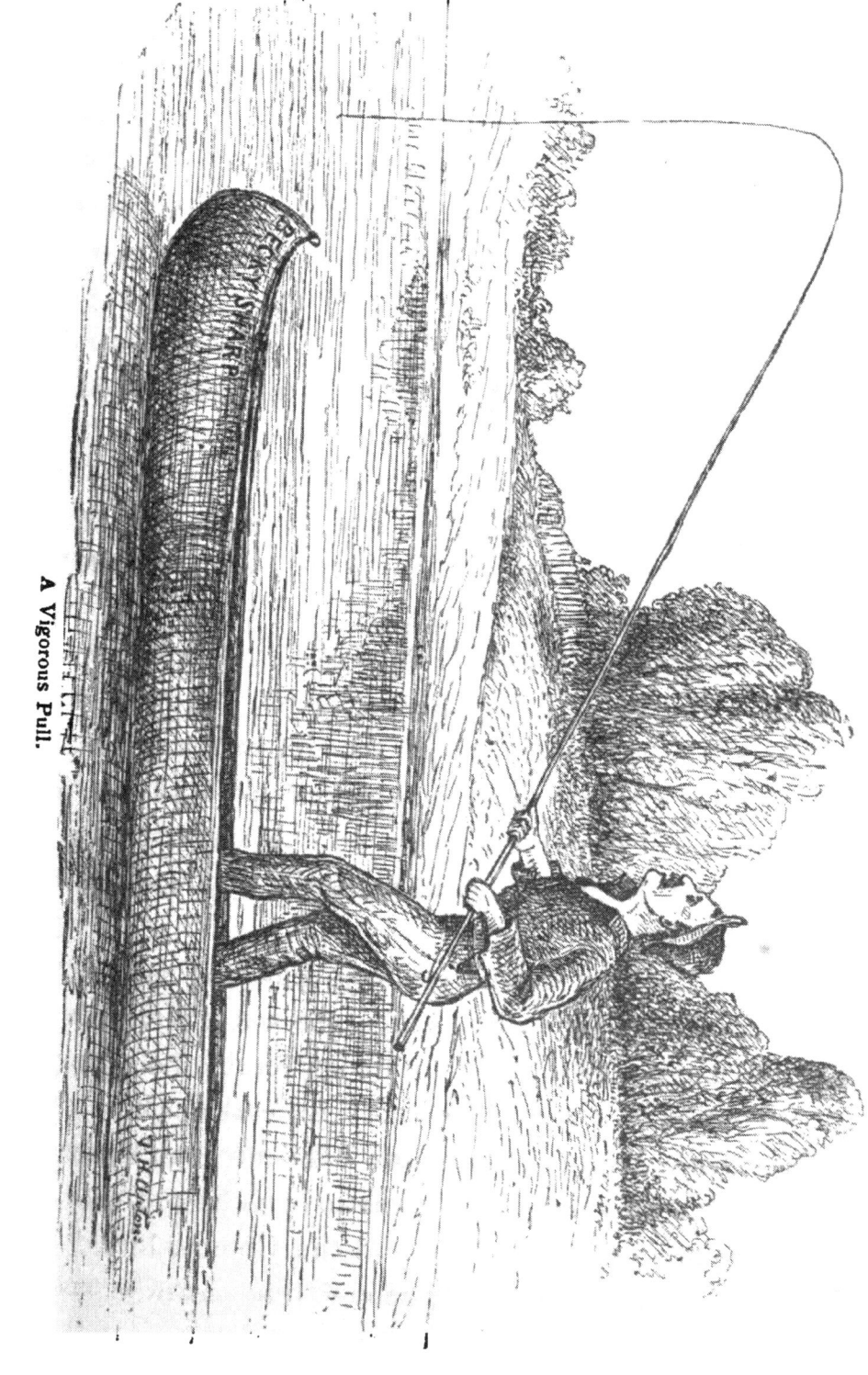

A Vigorous Pull.

rowed her and the Commodore's rod, and pushed out a few yards from the beach. Then rising gingerly to his feet he made one or two gentle casts with great circumspection and was about to claim his wager, but thinking to perfect his claim, made a third cast, which was a thought too vigorous. (*Result shown on page* 65.)

The flag ship was still afloat, and the Commodore being anxious about his rod, sprang aboard and pushed off to the rescue, but the Vice sternly waved him back.

"You may take your rod, if you like," said he, "though I could manage that too well enough, but I'll show you another point of superiority in a Chrysalid."

The Commodore took the rod and backed off to a respectful distance. The Arethusela had righted herself instantly after discharging her occupant, and floated full of water, but still buoyant from the air in her large watertight compartments. The Vice picked up his paddle, and put it aboard and then swam to the stern, which he grasped with both hands, and managed by a sudden and judicious effort to mount.

Then, hitching carefully along, leap-frog fashion, he was soon seated amidships, bailing the water out with his hat, the canoe still floating with considerable buoyancy.

"That is well done," was the general verdict. "A Chrysalid's water-tights are more efficient than those of a Red Laker provided she has any to bless herself withal."

"I want to take a bath," said the Commodore, "before turning in, and as a long enough time has now passed

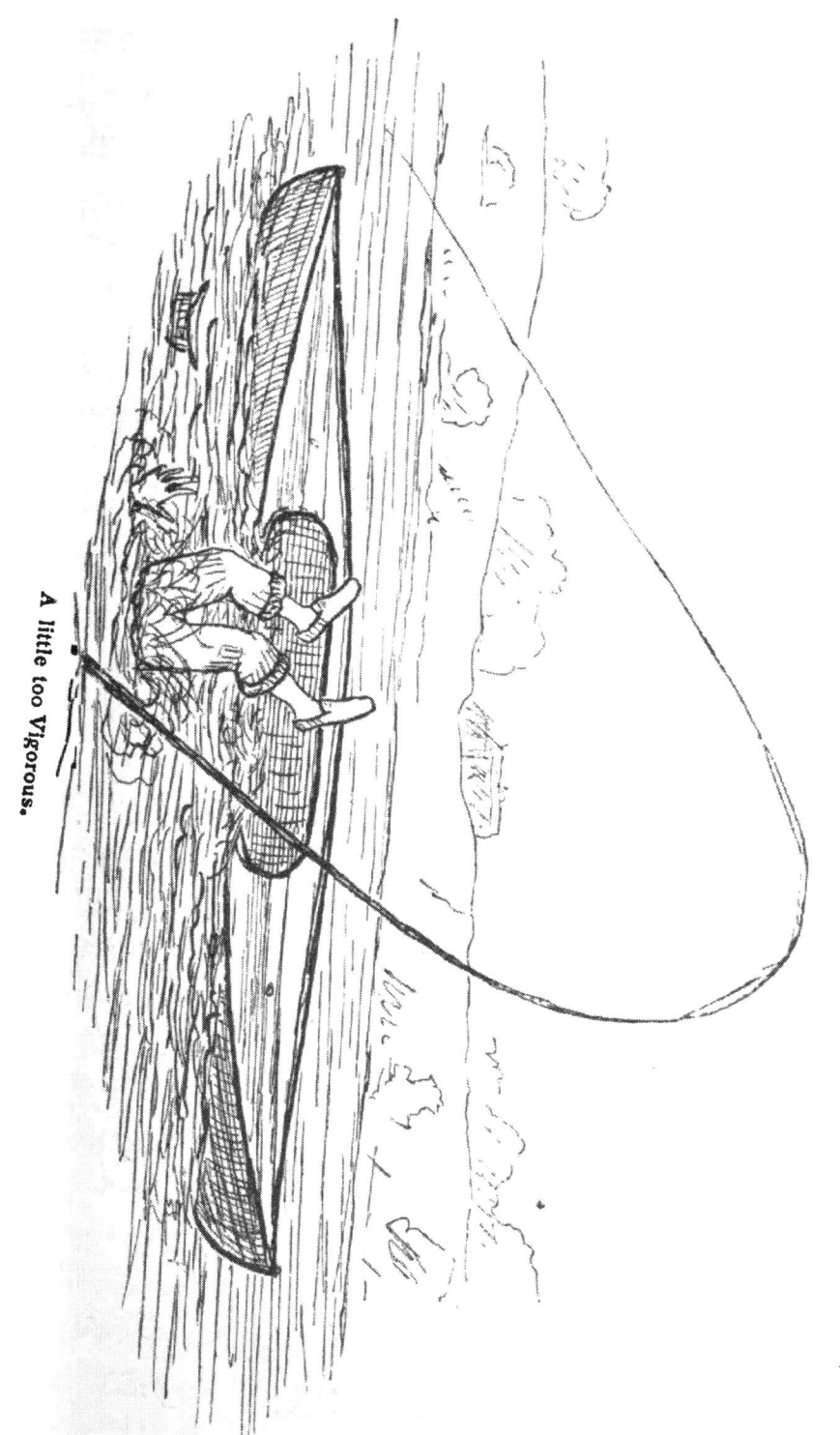

A little too Vigorous.

since supper to reasonably warrant exemption from congestion, I think I will test my water-tights if the Vice will permit me so to denominate the bags which serve in

Aquatic Leap-frog.

that capacity on board the flag ship. At any rate, I will prove to you that I can climb aboard a Red Laker without upsetting. I take precautions, you see, against wetting my toggery."

So saying the Commodore stripped, embarked, and when in deep water jumped overboard, climbing on board just as the Vice had done, and with about the same ease. Then he sat on the gunwale and upset his boat, filling her with water. She floated, but by no means so buoyantly as had the Arethusela, and the task of climbing on board was somewhat more critical as the power of flotation was so much less. However, the water being perfectly smooth, it was accomplished, and it is probable that the Commodore could have bailed her out without going ashore, if he had given time enough to the operation, and darkness had not come on. As it was, he prudently and laboriously paddled the water-logged flag ship ashore, where all hands performed their evening toilettes, and sat down around the camp fire to enjoy cigars, which the Vice had promptly handed over to the Cook, remarking that he did so under protest and stipulating that no precedent should thereby be established: "For," said he, "I laid a **wager** that I could throw a line while standing in the boat, and no fair-minded man can say I didn't do it."

With the moan of a rising gale in their ears, the members of the expedition soon dropped off to sleep.

IV.

THE WRECK OF THE ROCHEFORT.

AT dawn the Purser arose and woke the camp with the blood-curdling cry, "The Rochefort is gone!" The rest, as soon as they could rub their eyes open, scanned the lake to leeward, but no trace of the missing canoe could be seen. The sky was grey with low driving clouds and the lake repeated the sombre hue, save when it broke into white before the southerly gale.

With ill concealed reluctance the Commodore offered to lend his darling Becky to the bereaved Statesman, who protested that the loss of an election was as nothing in comparison with his present affliction. It must be admitted, too, that his remarks as to going in a Red Laker to the rescue of a Chrysalid, were not altogether gracious. However, the Purser volunteered to go with him in search of the runaway, each man following one side of the lake which was here only about two miles wide. Under the shortest possible sail, then, they set out, each standing across the wind at first, so as to close in with the shore and then follow it down with the wind astern. They went merrily off riding the white caps like ducks, and turning to follow the dark wooded shores to the North.

Presently the Purser was observed to broach to, and after a short time he went ashore, unshipped his mast and proceeded under paddle. It subsequently transpired that the sea wrenched off one of the "gudgeons" which held the rudder, and he was thereupon disabled for sailing purposes. The wind, however, was dead astern, and he progressed almost as easily and as fast as if he had not lost his helm.

Meanwhile the Vice proceeded, anxiously scanning the coast, and at length had the pleasure of discovering the

"His Ship she was a-wrack."

runaway some three miles down the lake, full of water, and with the sea, in dear old Robinson Crusoe's immortal words, "making a clean breach over her." That she was not stove into match-wood speaks well for her builder's workmanship. She had carried her anchor with her all the way, having been hove so short that she gradually worked off the steep beach as the wind and sea rose, and had not even cable enough out to anchor her off the lee shore on which she finally brought up.

As the Vice approached her, the buoyant Red-Laker rising cork-like with him on the white capped waves, he could not but be struck by the ship-shape appearance of the wreck. As has been intimated, the Vice is distinguished for elaboration of equipment, and he had anchored his canoe the night before with her sails beautifully furled, and every strand of her multitudinous running rigging exactly in position. Now she looked for all the world like a miniature frigate cast away on a rocky coast, and the solitary spectator half expected to discover a crew of pigmies clinging to her hatch-combings, as he drew near.

The first thing to be done however, was to signal the Purser, who was coasting the opposite shore. To beach his borrowed boat with such a sea running, and where there was not any beach but boulders, was a problem which might easily have floored the greatest statesman, but the Commodore is glad to certify, that the task was accomplished with due regard for the welfare of the flagship, and this while the Vice's own beloved Rochefort was perhaps banging herself to pieces on the boulders.

By dint of firing his revolver and waving his dandy, unshipped for the purpose, he succeeded in attracting the Purser's attention, and saw him change his course. This done, he waded to the stranded Rochefort, expecting to find her hopelessly broken amidships, but on getting her off the rocks, she floated as well as ever, showing that her compartments were still uninjured; so, anchoring her in waist-deep water, with her head to the sea, the Vice proceeded to bail.

Why this amber hue of the water? Alas, the Vice carried the coffee of the fleet and it was not in a water-tight box. Why this slight saccharine quality? Alas again, the Vice carried the expeditionary sugar. The coffee did not prove a total loss. Persistent boiling extracted from it a passable beverage, which served until a market town was reached, but the sugar was past redemption.

By the time the Purser had reached the scene of disaster the wreck was pumped dry, and careful inspection showed that she was wholly uninjured save as regards a few bruises. So the Vice unshipped her masts, and rightly judging that the Becky Sharp would be the easiest to tow, made fast her painter, and started on the long paddle against the wind back to camp.

To the rest of the fleet this escapade argued poor seamanship on the part of the Vice, but to him it only proved the moral obliquity of his boat. In order to shield his own reputation, he ruthlessly alleged against her the most abominable nautical crimes, and would never trust her alone thereafter, unless she was tied to a large tree or a huge boulder.

The Purser, meanwhile, noting the shoreward trend of the waves, instituted a successful search for his lost rudder, which he found ashore in a quiet cove. On returning to camp, he and the Vice admitted that there are certain advantages connected with a steering oar, which do not belong to a rudder, and each resolved thereafter to carry a suitable row-lock, so as not to be entirely disabled for sailing in case of accidents. Nevertheless, while a rudder holds, it is certainly more convenient than a paddle to steer with, but at the same time it necessitates an awkward amount of stern-post, which renders the boat hard to turn, and has usually to be shipped and unshipped in changing from sail to paddle. For this reason the Vice is accustomed to remark, that it is always well to have another fellow at hand in a Red-Laker to render aid in emergencies. Of course it was necessary to dry the Rochefort before proceeding, and it was afternoon before the Purser had repaired his steering gear, and everything was in readiness. There is always enough to do however, so all hands busied themselves in sundry tinkerings until after dinner, when, as the sky had cleared and the wind had somewhat moderated, the order was given to make sail, and the pretty island was speedily left behind, the fleet skimming along the wooded shore like a flock of white sea gulls.

Now whatever advantages a Chrysalid may possess over and above a Red-Laker, she is nowhere in point of speed on a free wind. Consequently the first division invariably ran away from the second, and was obliged every little while to lie by and wait for it to come up. After his first experience in jibing, the Cook had been content for awhile to trust to a spruce breeze, and indeed there had been since his overturn no favoring wind until now. He soon acquired commendable skill in laying a straight course. He no longer zig-zagged over the lake as at first. Evidently, however, something weighed upon his mind, for as with his companion boat he entered a bay to wait for the second division:

"Commodore," said he.

"Well?"

"I say, what *is* tacking anyhow?"

"Why it's working to windward."

"Yes, I know, but how do you do it?"

"O, I see. You don't understand the theory of sailing a boat. Well, I must own you're a plucky one. And you've done mighty well too."

Then the Commodore made his companion lie to, while the flag-ship worked past him to windward by short tacks. The Cook with his usual aptitude soon caught the idea and satisfactorily put it in practice. Then, as the breeze was moderate, there followed lessons in "jibing" and "wearing," with explanations of the circumstances under which each was necessary.

By the time the second division rounded the point, the Cook's spirits had risen, and he began once more to prate of his piratical ancestry who knew no home but the ocean.

"What were you two benighted Red Lakers doing

in the bay this side of Black Point?" asked the Vice as the party sat by the fire that evening.

"Merely a little discussion as to merits of rig, and the best way of handling a boat, with practical illustrations," said the Cook, who clung frantically to the remnant of his reputation for seamanship, and trusted to the Commodore's magnanimity not to expose him.

"O, that was it, eh? And what conclusions did you reach with your Red Lake monstrosities?"

"We had plenty of time to reach any conclusions, and have them illustrated and published, and sell a dozen editions before you came along," retorted the Cook.

"We were trying experiments," said the Commodore adroitly, "in going about, and we concluded that the best way was to come up into the wind as sharp as you like, hauling in a little on the dandy sheet to help, and then as soon as the mainsail shivers, give her one or two strokes with the paddle, let go your dandy sheet, hold your boom over till the mainsail fills, and her head falls off, shift your paddle to the lee side and there you are."

"Yes," said the Vice, who is a devoted adherent of a "sliding gunter" rig with full boom and gaff, standing lug, dandy, jib and flying jib, as distinguished from the two leg-of-mutton sails carried by the Red Lakers. "Yes, there you are indeed with your steering paddle and other unseamanlike contrivances. Now let me show you how a Chrysalid goes about. We will suppose this log to be the canoe."

"Parallel exact, so far," broke in the Cook, "Go ahead." Taking no notice of the interruption the Vice proceeded, seating himself astride the log,

"We will suppose the canoe to be under full sail on the port tack, with everything drawing. Order is given 'ready about,' crew spring to stations. Helmsman gives her a good full, passes port tiller-rope over his shoulder, takes it in his teeth and has his paddle handy. Let go flying jib halyards, and in with your down haul. Let go main sheet, and if you get a chance, haul in a little on the dandy. Round with your helm. When the mainsail begins to shiver, top your boom or lift it clear while she swings. If she don't come round, help her with your paddle. Let go dandy sheet if you hauled in on it. Let go topping lift, slack away weather jib sheet as soon as she is pointed on starboard tack. Bowse in flying jib halyards, letting mainsail take care of itself, make all fast, haul in main sheet, and there you are all ship-shape."

"And hull down astern of the Red Lakers," added the Commodore.

During this explanation the Vice had, after his own enthusiastic fashion, gone through all the motions, as he described them, and when he appealed to his auditors to know if it was not a far more artistic performance than that which the Commodore described, no one had a word to say.

"Just tell us, Vice," said the Cook, "how many ropes have you to attend to?"

"O there are only a few," responded the Vice, curiously enough not seeing the trap into which he was falling, "There are the dandy halyards, sheet and brail, that's three, main halyards—peak and throat—sheet, brail, and topmast halyards, that's seven, jib halyards, down haul, outhaul and sheets, that's twelve. Flying jib ditto ditto, that's seventeen. Tiller ropes and painter, that's all, total twenty. Oh, yes, and there's the signal halyards, that's twenty-two, or twenty-three if you have a pair on your topmast."

"He does get ahead of us, that's a fact, Commodore," drawled the Cook. "Now I can only make out two halyards, two sheets and a painter, five in all, unless I count my fish-line, and he has twenty-three. I give it up."

"Yes," said the Vice musingly, "when you are in a Chrysalid canoe, properly rigged, you have a sense of completeness, not to be attained elsewhere." Then suddenly changing the subject:

"I thought," said he, as he helped himself to an eighth slice of toast, "that I was lucky when the Cook kindly volunteered to carry my tent as a seat, and thus relieve my boat from a certain amount of weight, but now I am wondering under what cover this expedition will sleep tonight." It so happened that the expedition had not yet felt the loss of their tent, having at the different camps chanced upon lean-tos and other adequate substitutes.

"When you lack information on any matter connected with canoeing," said the Cook, "come to me." The Cook emptied his third cup (pint) of coffee, unrolled a pack in his boat, and displayed a piece of stout sheeting, five yards long and two and three-quarter yards wide, with four rope loops at each end for tent pins, and a row of button-holes, a foot apart, along each edge. He also dis-

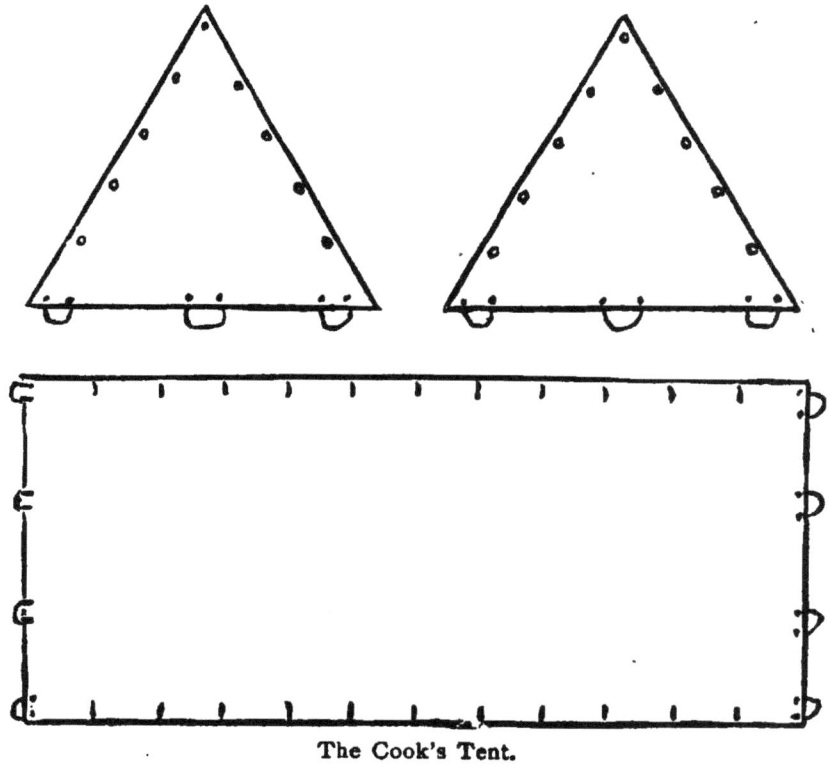

The Cook's Tent.

played two triangular pieces of the same material, at the bases of each of which were three loops for pins, and along the other two sides a row of buttons.

"Button these together properly," said he, "set the whole affair up on poles, and cross pole, or across a rope strung tightly between two trees, and you have a larger and better ventilated tent than the one I left in the lake;

it won't weigh half as much, either. Except in very cold weather or driving rain, the end pieces will not be neces-

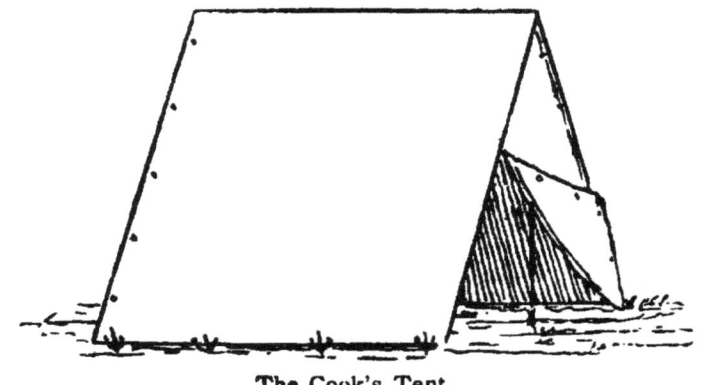

The Cook's Tent.

sary. Indeed, it can be set over a canoe, so as to cover all the open portion of the boat."

The whole supper table gazed admiringly, until the Commodore asked,

"Why have the holes, instead of the buttons, on the main piece."

"So that you may affix the ends either from the inside or outside. The latter is the easier way, but occasionally the wind blowing from the front, will come in very freely between the fastenings outside, so that the canoeist who drops asleep with a head full of pleasant dreams, will awake with a head full of neuralgia."

"And if it rains, what is to prevent this tent from leaking like a sieve, and distributing shower baths impartially among the clean and the unclean?"

"Two things—a steep pitch or a neat coat of oil," said the Cook.

"The water-proof of the pudding is in the eating," remarked the Commodore, who had begun to yawn. "Set the tent at once."

The tent was set on a line between two trees, the front remaining open, and half an hour later there lay within it four men who were beginning fully to realize how delicious weariness may become, when it is earned by the body instead of the brain. With sand for matresses, and a rubber blanket each for sheets, they slept more soundly than they had ever done at home upon springs and between linen. The only visitations they experienced were heavenly ones. Venus glided past the open front, but saw no one there over whom her fastidious gaze cared to linger. Saturn peeped suspiciously in, but passed on contentedly, assured that in the presence of such sound sleepers his rings were as safe as if they were Indian Rings at Washington. Mars glared in with his great red face, but the quartette had been all day on the water, under an unfamiliar sun, so there were four fiery faces to Mars' one, and the blazing old fellow went off in a huff and got behind a little cloud to hide his mortification.

V.

SUNSHINE AND SHADOW.

IF the reader has watched with any interest, the development of what may perhaps without offence be termed canoebial character, he must have been pained to observe that however fair minded the average canoeist may be in other respects, neither his judgment nor his statements can be trusted where his own boat is concerned. Of this fact each member of the expedition became convinced in the course of the first day out, and the authors deem it their duty to warn the public against indiscriminate belief in the virtues ascribed to different canoes by their respective owners.* The Statesman, who has associated to some extent with sporting men, says, that he has observed a like trait in owners of horses, dogs

---

* NOTE.—The ~~Cook~~ [Commodore] wishes it to be understood that all his statements regarding the ~~Cherub~~ [Becky Sharp] are strictly truthful, but really when ~~Commodore~~ [Cook] says that the ~~Becky Sharp~~ [Cherub]—Well, space will not admit of specifications.

Hurray! I had the last look at *that* proof.

COMMODORE.

and yachts, and all know that every mother discovers in her own children beauties and virtues which no other living being is able to perceive. Why then, should a trait which is beautiful in one case be scoffed at in another? The authors hold that a sublime faith in one's own canoe, is one of the noblest sentiments that can animate the human breast.

Morning opened with the usual brisk breeze ruffling the lake from the south, and the fleet made all preparations to continue the voyage under sail. Hardly, however, were they clear of the land when the wind fell suddenly, and in a wonderfully short space of time the lake was like a mill pond. An occasional puff of wind however, justified keeping sails set, and so alternating from paddle to canvas, a broad expanse was passed, and the "narrows" neared where mountains seemed trying to shoulder one another into the lake, and where, as if they had fallen off in the scuffle, several rocky, wood-crowned islands floated double as it were, on the glassy water. By the time the shadow of the woods was reached, all hands were glad to stop until the declining sun should make motion a little more endurable, so a cool and shady nook was selected where several hours were spent in meditative contemplation of as lovely a panorama as ever rested the eyes of leisurely voyagers.

This *laisser aller* fashion of cruising is the only really enjoyable plan. Your restless spirits will push on and make their twenty-five miles a day, rain or shine, but your philosopher is content it may be with five or six, and recks not if he be obliged to cut his journey short at its latter end. So the hours drifted slowly by until the mountains threw their shadows across the lake, and a gentle breeze once more invited action.

It took only an hour or two to run out from the shadow of the mountain range, and see stretching out toward the north the low lying hills which characterize the broad St. Lawrence Valley, for thitherward tend in the Canadas all waters that run down hill. The lake, too, spread out again, its edges bordered by extensive shallows whereon grew tall graceful bulrushes, each of which rose six or eight feet or more above the water, tapering beautifully and smoothly from near an inch in diameter at the base, to a needle-like point at the top. Sometimes when the wind was fresh, the cruisers would run in among them. There was something peculiarly fascinating in thus flying through vast green stretches of rustling, bending reeds. The breeze was almost wholly checked near the water, but the peaks of the sails caught it above the supple rushes, and the canoes went whistling through them, their sharp bows dividing the green stems as they flew along, and a broad swath bowing under the booms as they swung out to leeward.

Now and then a startled marsh hen, or wild fowl of some sort, would rise almost from under the gunwales and go scuttling off, frightened half to death at the unwonted invasion of her retreat. The solitude was perfect.

The canoeists could see nothing of one another when separated by a few yards. Any one might have upset and

"Green grow the Rushes, oh!"

been left far behind, before the rest could have discovered his loss, and then the chance of ever finding him would have been as one to a hundred. However the water was only two or three feet deep, so that there was no actual danger. Along such tracts as this the fleet coasted this afternoon, and there was no apparent prospect of getting beyond, or through the reeds to find a camp. The lake was wide, and it was not expedient to cross it so near night-fall, and with a threatening sky. So sails were prudently furled and the four cruisers paddled along hoping to find, somewhere, an opening through which the land could be reached. The sky grew dark. Rain began to plash around, and suddenly night shut down, with a cold driving mist and not a glimmer of light to show the bearings, save an occasional momentary gleam from one of the little light-houses away off toward the north. The fleet had drawn out into the lake in order to get a better sight at the coast line, and here it rode with the heaving water all around, and no means of steering to a place of safety. The Vice had taken the bearings with his compass, but now as fast as a lantern was lighted to steer by, the wind blew it out, so there was nothing for it but keep together, and steer by the sea. After a somewhat anxious time, with startling suddenness, a long dark wall seemed to rise through the rain and drive straight forward over the lake. "Hold all" was the word for a moment, but there was no roar of surf, only a whistling murmur as of a million wings. Then the dark wall opened and the reeds were recognized as old friends. The course in which the fleet was heading, had been entirely problematical, for the wind was very gusty and variable, but it was certain that among the countless slender stems was safety from the fiercest gale that ever blew. Pushing inward for a hundred yards or so, the boats were moored side by side, to sheaves of reeds, and their occupants proceeded to make themselves as comfortable as was possible under the circumstances, feeling, as the Cook remarked, better able than ever before to appreciate the early experiences of Moses.

Now, if ever, was the time to try the Purser's "Rob Roy cuisine." He had imported it at great outlay of treasure from England and had repeatedly explained its beauties, but having received it just on the eve of departure from New York, he had never practically tested its virtues, and the professional prejudices of the Cook were so obstinately in favor of a wood fire, that he could never be persuaded to use a substitute. This "cuisine" is a canoeing device invented by Mr. Macgregor, the father of modern canoeing. In external appearance it is a circular box of plated copper. The main part of the box is used as a stew-pan, the top as a frying-pan. Moreover it contains, compactly fitted, an alcohol blast-lamp, and a multitude of little cooking contrivances which are admirable under circumstances like those in which the command was now placed. The Purser knew by heart the theoretical rules for managing the cuisine, but as has been stated, had never put them in practice.

By the light of the little lanterns, he now took out the compact apparatus, opened it, filled the lamp, placed the standard on his forward deck, struck a match and applied it to the aperture. An innocent, bluish flame appeared, flickered for a moment, gathered strength, burst into a roar, shot upward three feet, shook itself, and prepared seemingly to consume the entire fleet. The Purser shrank backward as far as the narrow limits of his Chrysalid would allow, and glared helplessly at the vicious little engine, while he made abortive efforts to reduce it to decorum. The rest shipped their cables and hauled off, leaving him to his fate.

"Kick it overboard."

"Put your hat on it."

"Blow it out."

"Douse that glim," were some of the directions shouted, as muskrats skurried away into the darkness, and an owl and one or two bats swooped within the circle of light to see what was up. But the Purser remembered the bill he had paid, and resolved to risk his life rather than lose his " cuisine."

As the roaring continued without abatement and with no disastrous results, it presently occurred to the Cook that here was a splendid heat going to waste. In a trice he had the coffee pot in position, and in a marvelously short time more each man had a cup of hot coffee and a rude sandwich, cut hap-hazard from a half soaked loaf. The Rob Roy cuisine was unanimously voted a success, where for any reason an ordinary fire cannot be lighted.

It is not pretended that a remarkably comfortable

night followed this episode, but it was much better than driving aimlessly before the wind on the lake, and most of the party managed to get some sleep under their rubber blankets. At any rate the expedition was safe, and its members could listen without concern to the gale that roared a few feet over their heads, but touched them not.

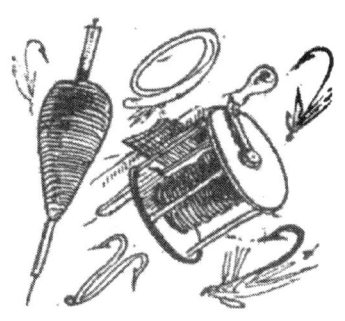

VI.

MY NATIVE LAND, FAREWELL.

MORNING dawned on a somewhat forlorn set of castaways. Every man was more or less damp, not to say wet, and the Vice with his bedraggled mutton-chop whiskers presented a peculiarly lugubrious appearance as he exasperated the Americans of the party by singing in the pitch of an Irish " keen " the old Southern air " Maryland, My Maryland."

The day promised to be a fair one, and by sunrise land had been reached, a fire built, dry clothes extracted from bags and water-tight compartments, and amiability once more asserted its mild and benignant sway over the depressed spirits of the command. This was the last day on the lake, although its lower end was on a small scale what the geographers might almost term a lacustrine river. It was broad, that is, and at times nearly currentless. The nominal division between lake and river, however, was marked by a railway bridge and here it was understood the fleet must stop for official recognition by her majesty's representative before crossing the Dominion line. The town lay low along the lake shore, and under the shelter of a wooden break-water the fleet successfully effected a landing. The Commodore, after a few moments spent in making himself look as respectable as possible, set off on his official visit to the British Consulate. As he departed, the Vice asked if the needed

"But the Consul's brow was sad."

stores were not to be purchased at this point, and before the expedition entered alien if not hostile waters.

"Of course not," said the Cook. "You can buy better things for half the money in Canada."

"Under a monarchical government," added the Purser.

"That is undoubtedly the best plan," said the Commodore.

"Now look here. I'm a citizen of the United States," began the Vice, but the Purser, the Cook and the Commodore fled in as many different directions and left him gesticulating solus upon the lonely shore.

Presently the Commodore returned, followed shortly by the British Consul, who wished to assure himself that the squadron was not the advance guard of a Fenian expedition. The Vice begged the right to receive him officially in the Commodore's stead, and this favor being granted, the Consul was treated to half an hour of impassioned eloquence upon the rights of man.

Meanwhile the breeze freshened and inflated itself to the size of a gale. Sloops and sail boats began to huddle together behind the little breakwater. The custom-house officer kindly offered to find a trusty guard for the canoes while their officers should go ashore, but the suggestion was declined with thanks. The Purser longed to be on British soil once more, the Vice was impatient to pat his own love of country on the back, by observing how much more miserably England's subjects exist than do those of his own happy land, the Commodore saw a fort in the distance, which he and the Cook, having once been soldiers, were impatient to inspect, and the Cook pined for Canada, because he understood that the expeditionary butter pail might there be more cheaply refilled. Then the humane custom-house officer appealed to their sense of personal safety, to their regard for the friends and creditors who might miss them if they were drowned, as they surely would be if they ventured out in such a storm. But the eye of Britannia was gazing upon the expedition from under the pith helmet of the Consul, so the Commodore roared,

"Prepare to pass bridge! Strike standing rigging! Club and private signals fore and aft!"

"One minute, Commodore," shouted the Vice, who was dancing frantically about his boat, "where shall I display the flag of Our Country?" And the Vice reverently drew a small American flag from his bosom.

"Display it in your pocket," replied the Commodore, rudely. "Forward!"

The Vice glared angrily, and got as far with a reply as to shout, "The Alderman always—" when the sight of the Cherub, the Arethusela and the Becky Sharp, dancing vivaciously on the big waves as their respective commanders plied their paddles rapidly, each with the intention of being the first to pass between the piles of the bridge and cross the Dominion line, caused the Vice to become inspired with the strongest sentiment acquired in the practice of statesmanship, namely, that nothing is so disastrous as to be left behind. The wind being directly abaft, there could be no possible doubt as to the fate of any commander or boat that might be dashed against the piles, particularly if he first got into the trough of the sea, and was cast up broadside. Each man braced himself, leaning warily forward, each paddle performed wondrous and unexpected gyrations in air, and the colors vanished and darted up again like guidons in a cavalry fight. The commodorial helmet was blown off at this juncture, and in recovering it the flag ship had fallen some distance to the rear. Noting this with some disgust, the Commodore successfully executed a tactical movement which redounded greatly to his own glory. He shouted,

"On, first division, deploy column. Squadron into line; Guide Right, March! (when manœuvering the squadron, the Commodore was everlastingly bothered by unbidden reminiscences of army tactics, which led him to enunciate orders applicable to the handling of a battalion instead of a fleet.)

The effect of this command was to subject the squadron to the moral influence of discipline; it was also to arrest for an instant the progress of the three boats which had distanced the Commodore's, for it was the flag-ship itself that was at the right, and upon this the squadron was to align itself. The principal effect was to give the wily Commodore the advantage of a boat's length. The Vice comprehended the trick only when it was too late, and the gnashing of his teeth could be distinctly heard above the whistling of the gale. But if distanced by trickery, he at least could console himself with patriotism, which is the last refuge of a Statesman.* Wildly he snatched the flag of his country from his pocket; proudly

* This was not the noun used by Dr. Johnson in his famous definition of patriotism.

he waved it aloft as the nose of his canoe shot safely between the piles. Gloriously the holy rag fluttered in the air for an instant; then it wrapped a fold about a huge oak splinter of one of the under-timbers of the bridge, which nearly dislocated the Vice's shoulder in passing. Then

The United States Garrison.

it concluded to remain where it was, and there it flutters to this day, to show to timorous mariners where the gallant Vice passed the bridge. As for the Vice himself, he dropped his paddle as he emerged, several lengths behind every body else, into the comparatively still water behind the bridge; then he rubbed his agonized shoulder, and remarked,

"Patriotism always *did* play the devil with Statesmen."

The squadron now drifted under the granite walls of a United States fort, which commanded the approaches from Her Majesty's dominions. It bore the marks of neglect usually seen in an unoccupied and unfinished fort, but as the canoes drew near, signs of life manifested themselves about the sally-port, and in less time than it takes to write it the entire garrison had embarked and was advancing to reconnoitre the approaching fleet. A parley ensued to the mutual edification of both parties,

The Purser on British Soil.

and then the race for the Dominion line was resumed and easily won by the Purser, who paddled into water so shoal that the mud was visible just below the surface. He turned his boat on her centre as rapidly as a man could do with a canoe of the Chrysalid pattern; then he arose and exclaimed, as the Vice and the Cook drew up,

"Gentlemen, this is the first time in eight years that I've stood upon British soil. 'God save the Queen!' say I, and three cheers"—

"You're not on British soil," interrupted the Vice;

"you're on British water." But the Purser, unmindful of the interruption, had got as far as "hip, hip!"—when the motion of raising his hat destroyed his equilibrium, and a second later he was more than knee deep in a hummock of greyish-blue mud.

"Now you're on British soil," continued the Vice; "how do you like it as far as you've got?"

But the unchanged ecstasy of the Purser's patriotic face banished from the hearts of his companions any memories of '76 and 1812 that might have been hiding there, and the three cheers were heartily given with a supplementary "tiger," which was fully as noisy as if it had been one of the tigers native to the royal lady's own Indian Empire.

The Purser extracted himself with some difficulty from his native clay, and all paddled to a shelving beach for the noontide rest, the Cook and the Commodore striking up "God save the Queen," out of compliment to the Purser. The others joined in and the notes of the noble old anthem rang far across the water until it was noticed that the Vice was patriotically roaring the words:

> "My Country 'tis of thee
> Sweet land of libertee,"

instead of the original. The other two Americans, although they were old United States soldiers, could not brook this gratuitous affront to their English companion, so they vigorously attacked the Vice with their paddles and spattered him till he was fain to cry "quarter."

Then the bows grated on the sand, and springing lightly ashore, the Vice mounted a boulder and delivered himself as follows, while the rest, dumb with amazement, sat in their boats to listen and applaud:

*"Far be it from me fellow-citiz —mariners, to disturb the harmony of this joyful occasion. We are gathered to-night almost upon the very spot where Chartreaux and Champlain and Vanjohn and Rouget Noir fit the Injuns and made them knuckle to the Jesuit Fathers, with none to molest nor make them afraid. Here subsequently Lord Howe and Commodore Vanderbilt marched their squadrons and manœuvered their battalions, and spliced the main brace, and shivered their timbers according to the dictates of their own consciences. Did any of them ever go back on their environment? No; contrariwise they harmonized, and shall we their successors fail to do likewise? Never, gentlemen, never. It has been hurled in our faces by the honorable gentleman from England, that the great republic is rotten with corruption—that our highest officers are not above peculation. Let me ask that honorable gentleman and his allies (here the Statesman indicated the Commodore and the Cook,) if any president of the United States ever stole corn meal and had his disgraceful act perpetuated in his country's literature? I pause for a reply. None? Then none has ever done such a deed. And yet, gentlemen, it is recorded of one of the most exemplary of Eng-

* Reported in full on the spot by the Editor.

lish monarchs that he not only stole the then current equivalent of corn meal, but caused it to be used on the royal table. I invite you to join me in singing a song to the glory of Old England—one, two, three: sing!

(Air Auld Lang Syne.)

When good King Arthur ruled this land,
  He was a goodly king.
He stole three pecks of barley meal,
  To make a bag-pudding.

A bag-pudding the Queen did make,
  And stuffed it well with plums,
And in it put great lumps of fat,
  As big as my two thumbs.

The King and Queen did eat thereof,
  And noblemen beside,
And what they could not eat that night,
  The Queen next morning fried.
                (Great applause.)

"Can anything more clearly indicate a low moral sentiment than the existence, and acknowledged popularity of this song? Fellow citizens (carried away by the tide of eloquence the Statesman forgot to say shipmates) and you, sir, whose alien friendship I am proud to own, although the unfortunate accident of a foreign birth (for which I cannot blame you,) opens a chasm between us—fellow citizens, I have done. My native land is behind me. I now appeal for protection to the Queen of England, and for the time being repudiate the American Eagle—though with all his faults I love him still."

Amid thunders of applause the Vice jumped down and inquired why luncheon was not ready.

After an hour's rest and refreshment in a sheltered nook, the squadron proceeded on its way under paddle, the wind having died out, making for a heavily wooded island visible several miles distant, on which it was surmised there would be good camping ground. Islands indeed proved to be the most satisfactory camping places that were found during the expedition, and were invariably selected when practicable.

The squadron paddled socially along, side by side, until the Cook stopped his stroke and fell behind. As he seemed to be engaged in making some not very satisfactory arrangement of his luggage, the Commodore ranged alongside and asked what was the matter.

"I can't fix my seat so as to be comfortable."

"Thought so."

"How do you fix yours?"

"Why this way," and the Commodore, vacated his seat, turning round and sitting on his forward thwart, so as to afford an unobstructed view. The two other canoes had now drawn near.

"Look at that," said the Vice. "He can stand up and turn round without upsetting in that old tub of his."

"So can I," said the Cook, suiting the action to the word.

"So cannot we," said the Purser, and the Vice. "But what are you looking at?"

It is a characteristic of Chrysalid canoeists that they never notice anything outside of their own boats until they bring up all standing, as it were, against it. Hence

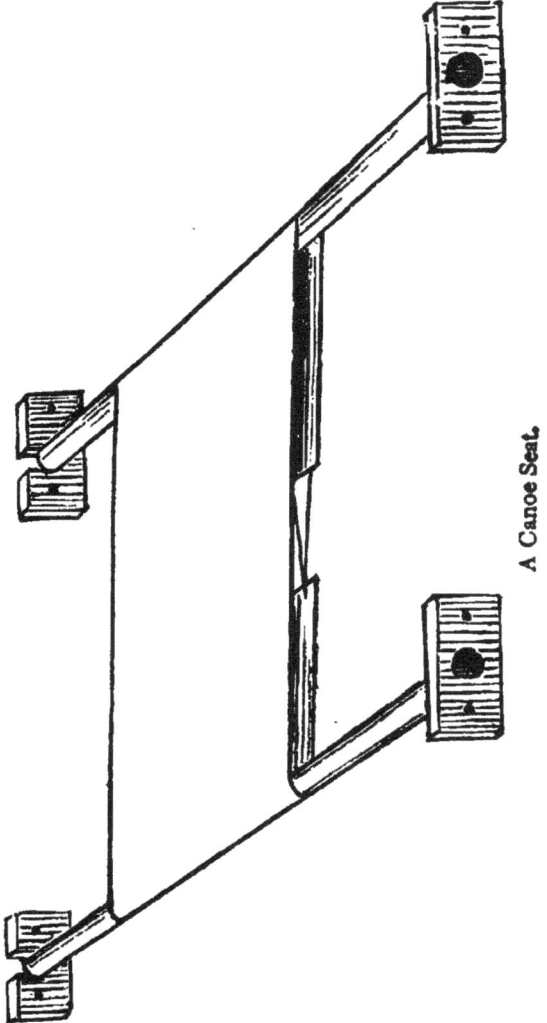

A Canoe Seat.

the Commodore's seat was a novelty to them, and they gazed upon it with mute admiration.

The blocks in which the cross-pieces rest, are screwed to the inside of the canoe. The cross-pieces are ash sticks about an inch in diameter. They are fourteen inches apart. Over and around them is passed a piece of fourteen inch canvas, with grommets for lacing on the under side. The seat should have a slight slope aft and should be so placed that a back-board will rest conveniently against the after thwart or bulkhead. If the cross-pieces spring too much, two bits of wood cut to fit between them on either side of the canvas will make the whole structure very firm and elastic. A simpler arrangement is a movable thwart made of half-inch pine, with cross-pieces tongued and grooved across the ends to prevent splitting. If made eighteen inches wide, such a thwart may be used for a lee-board, as the canoeist should sit on or near the bottom of his craft when under canvas.

"There are some advantages about Red Lake canoes," said the Vice.

"Very plebeian though," said the Cook, satirically; "their principal mission is to go cruising with Chrysalids in the capacity of tenders."

"Yes," said the Vice, "I admit their carrying capacity."

"And their superior speed," said the Cook.

"And their great stability," added the Commodore. So with cheerful chaff the fleet went on its way, and in a couple of hours was making camp on a pretty island, evidently a resort for picnickers and which was playfully called "Murderer's Isle," from an unpleasant episode of early days.

The Commodore, having noted an abundance of drift

lying about, detailed himself to procure fire-wood, and stretched at full length upon the dry sand, leisurely tossed fragments of wood toward the spot where the Cook was engaged in the soothing attempt to light a fire with damp paper and wet matches, and the Purser was scraping, within the water's edge, a hole to be used after supper as a dish-pan, when the expedition suddenly obtained its first foreign view of the picturesque. From the shore of the main land there crept out something which at first bore itself somewhat as indicated on the next page.

It finally resolved itself into a strange craft which seemed to be a generous pig-trough remodelled by one with yearnings after the art of the undertaker. Standing, yet bent nearly double, in the stern was a slight, short old man, clothed in raiment utterly unlike anything which any member of the expedition had ever seen at home. The old man paddled his boat at a surprising rate of speed directly toward the camp of the expedition, and as he did so the gazers gradually

The Picturesque afar.

lost their enjoyment of the picturesque in the realization of a dread duty about to devolve upon them for the first time during the cruise. The old man being a Canadian, it naturally resulted that he must be a Frenchman, and incapable of English. Who was to converse with him? The Cook, who had picked up some French among the Louisiana creoles, but had not for ten years heard or

The Picturesque anear.

spoken a word of the beautiful language, modestly retired behind the Commodore's broad shoulders. The silence began to be terrible, but it was bliss compared with the sensation with which the group shuddered when the strange craft slid noiselessly and darkly up the beach, and her crew partially undoubled himself and remarked,

"Wahu ei hoo mi eh ha ma?"

"Three mariners involuntarily dropped back a pace or two; the fourth (the Cook) felt secure in his inconspicuousness until he discovered that he had been dropped to the ground by the Commodore's backward movement, and that the Commodore was nervelessly sitting upon him. At length the Vice, whose admiration for the French Commune had caused him to immure himself many a night with some ex-Communists who had escaped to America, asked in faltering tones,

"Q'est-ce-que vous voulez?"

"That's it," gasped the Cook, as he endeavored to

reanimate the Commodore's spinal cord with the sharp end of a quill toothpick, "make the ancient mariner explain himself."

But the Ancient Mariner only shook his head with a vague look, and said,

Wahu ei hoo mi eh ha ma?

"O hyu wuh oo mi en?"

Then the Commodore, who had lived a year in Paris, and was familiar with the polite phrases there in vogue, said,

"Voulez-vous pourboire?"

The old man shook his head, scrutinized the party closely, read the names of the boats, and exclaimed,

"Haw hihi."

Then the Purser, who before he left Oxford had made a French translation of the "Antigone" of Sophocles, which competent judges pronounced superior to that of Voltaire, stepped a pace to the front to hide his blanched countenance, and said,

"Nous ne comprenons pas."

And the old man replied,

"Haw hihi, hahu?"

By this time the Cook, who had extricated himself from beneath the ruins of the Commodore, was discreetly and rapidly seeking the leafy coverts of the forest, but the Vice detected him and dragged him back. The Cook put on an air of bravery and exclaimed,

"It's no use, boys; I'm convinced that he's a Basque, who has strayed up into France, and somehow got over here. I speak half a dozen languages, but there are no affinities between the Basque and any other known dialect. It will be just as well to talk English to him as anything else, so here goes. Say, old friend, we don't know what you're driving at, but"—here a happy thought struck the Cook, "say it over again." And while the Cook listened attentively, the old man repeated his first inquiry,

"Wahu ei hoo mi eh ha ma?"

"Certainly!" exclaimed the Cook briskly, "how much do you ask for them?"

"Hihi heh," replied the old man with great animation.

"It's a bargain," said the Cook; "Purser, please give the ancient mariner half a dollar?" And then the Cook, with the air of a man who comprehended the wisdom of the ages, explained to his astonished auditors. "Gentlemen, our visitor is not a Frenchman at all; he is an Irishman whose palate has departed, and he wants to know if we will buy two pike and a bass—'hoo mi eh ha ma,'—you know." The old man in the meantime hurried to his boat, paddled off to a crate anchored on the edge of the channel, and returned with a string of fish in the full vigor of life.

The three linguists sat deliberately down upon the sand, and their lips remained closed until coaxed from their obduracy by the mingled odors of coffee, fried fish, buttered toast and canned peaches. The Vice was heard to mutter, "French I can talk and most patois I can understand, but Basque complicated with loss of palate throws me." Presently however he began to exhibit symptoms of his accustomed loquacity.

It so happened that the supper table was sustained by resting against the cut-water of the Cherub, and it gradually dawned upon the Vice that there was something peculiar about her construction, something, that is, different from the construction of a Chrysalid which

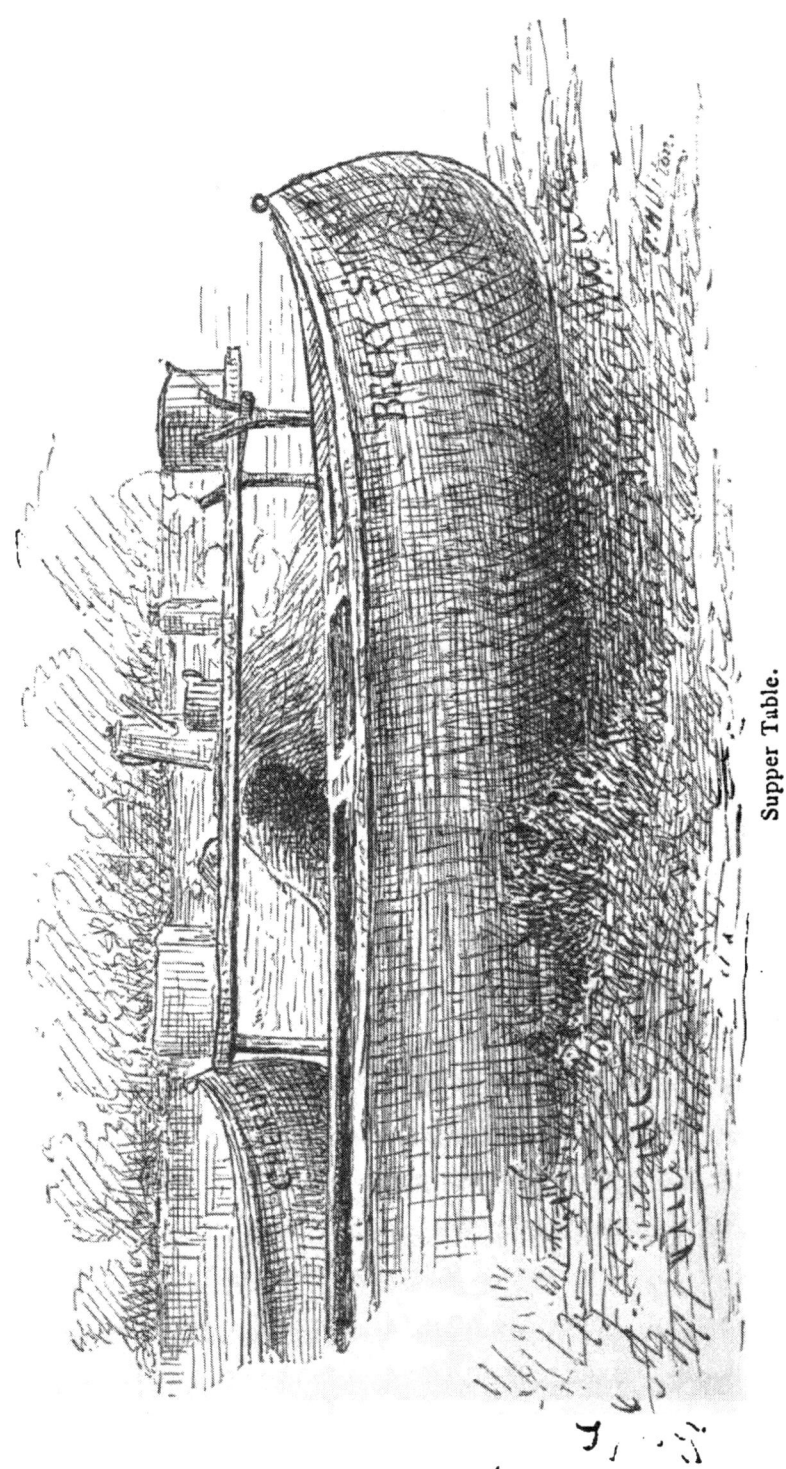

Supper Table.

which is built in the orthodox style, known as lap-streak or clinker, the planks being of quarter-inch white cedar, and the timbers of well seasoned oak. Said he, addressing the owners of the Red Lakers:

" Why don't the joints between your planking show?"

" Because the boats are not built in that way," said the Cook.

" But that's no way to build a boat ; the seams can't be made tight unless the planks over-lap. Look at the Rochefort."

" Very true," said the Commodore, " but our boats don't seem to leak so very much more than yours do, for all that."

" How are they built any how?" and the Purser and the Vice simultaneously arose and examined the Red Lakers by moonlight and firelight.

Mention has already been made of the characteristic indifference of Chrysalid owners to all canoes which are not Chrysalids until some chance occurrence forces them to make examination.

In this respect they strikingly resemble certain ecclesiastical sects, which rest serenely ignorant of other denominations, until they stumble upon information inadvertently, which startles into respectful investigation.

" Why they are perfectly smooth inside and out,"— " no timbers at all,"—" what lots of rivets," were some of the remarks.

" Certainly, haven't we told you so a dozen times,"

said the Cook, "and you never looked at them before."

"How do you suppose they are made?" asked the Vice.

"I am informed," replied the Commodore, "that thin strips of white cedar are steamed and bent transversely over an exact model or "last" of the intended canoe. The edges are straight so that they fit closely against one another. When all these are in place, a longitudinal outside sheathing of cedar or other wood, butternut in the case of our boats, is copper-fastened to the inner lining, the nails being driven through both thicknesses at short intervals, and clinched on the inside. The ribs and sheathing as used by the builder are each a quarter-inch thick, so that the total thickness is half an inch. The canoe is perfectly free from ribs inside, and from the raised edges outside, and cannot leak while she remains sound. Her strength is necessarily immense from the way in which she is put together."

"I think," added the Cook, "that we get a good deal of speed out of this model from the absence of the overlaps which are unavoidable in clinker built boats. These necessarily hold the water to an extent which must be appreciable in so light a craft. Moreover, the fore and aft curve of the bottom line rids them of a deal of what builders call 'skin-friction.' Recent experiments indicate that a shape like the bowl of a spoon offers the least resistance in passing over the surface of water."

"Your boats approximate to the spoon shape, that's a fact," said the Purser.

"Look at those rivets," remarked the Vice, "they make her look as though she were freckled."

"Granted," was the Cook's answer, "but are not freckles beautiful when they indicate a sound constitution?"

"The rib-and-batten, and the paper boats are quite as smooth outside," the Commodore admitted, "but, they all have internal projections which are sometimes inconvenient, as for instance when you wish to sleep on board, or when you are trying to sponge out sand and so forth."

The Purser and the Vice closed the dispute by proving that their lap-streak cedar boats when empty were somewhat lighter than the others, and the Commodore and Cook were fain to be content with asserting that if lightness were the only object, Red-Lakers could be built lighter than Chrysalids by using thinner stuff.

VII.

GARRISON LIFE.

THE Vice and the Purser, having boats of the Chrysalid model, were so long in stowing their cargoes that the Commodore and the Cook started in advance of the remainder of the squadron and made a brisk run to a British fort, the outline of whose parapet was discernible to a military eye, on an island some miles distant. When built during the last war, this work was far beyond the range of Yankee guns, but now the two forts might exchange cards with some chance of doing execution, albeit they are out of sight of one another.

Doubting what reception they might meet at the hands of a British garrison, the voyagers resolved themselves into two divisions, one of which approached the water-gate, while the other ran behind a stockade which flanked the work. No sentries being visible upon the parapet, the two officers disembarked and having learned in former days never incautiously to approach an earthwork, they advanced up the glacis and along the counterscarp with due circumspection. Suddenly the Cook paused, seized his companion's arm; struck a dramatic attitude and exclaimed,

An Unknown Fortress.

"Behold the garrison!"

The couple, who had walked as they conversed, had reached one of the bastions, and as the Cook spoke, the two men beheld, between the gabion-lined walls of an embrasure, three children with uncovered heads and saucer-like eyes.

"'Grim-visaged war hath smoothed his wrinkled front,'" said the Cook.

"'And thus be it ever,'" quoted the Commodore.

By this time the Purser and the Vice had made the island, and joined the first arrivals, who carefully and with professional pride inspected the outward defences of the fort, using technical military terms with a fluency which humbled their civilian companions into comparative silence. At length the Vice, noticing the rotting stockade, the weedy ditch, and other signs of inattention, ventured to let the eagle scream a note or two.

"Just like everything else, that is subject to the decaying influence of monarchical institutions," said he. "How quickly a handful of our brave fellows would take possession of it!"

"Perhaps," admitted the Commodore, "but I'd prefer to risk my chances from the inside."

The Purser immediately patted the Commodore on the back, while the Vice opened his eyes and demanded an explanation.

"Some forts," remarked the Commodore, "are like singed cats; they fight better than they look. This fort is in better condition now, than half the forts were that have become historic."

"But in case of sudden war," said the Vice, "there's nothing at hand to repair a broken-down fort with, is there?"

"Yes; living men; they make and unmake forts," said the Commodore brusquely.

"It's the same way with conventions and caucuses," remarked the Vice, regaining his self-respect as he imagined himself once more the Commodore's equal.

"You've been a soldier," said the Purser to the Cook, "and I am longing to see once more the uniform of my native country. Tell me how to gain admission to the fort."

The Cook replied,

"Go around to the sally port, which you will be sure to find opening away from the neighboring republic, and fire your pistol. The guard will hurry out and make you its prisoner; then the Commodore and I will come around and intercede for you, on the ground of your ignorance."

The Purser looked disdainful; "And think you," said he, "that Britain's laws are so fitful as to waver under the persuasions of a brace of Yankees?"

"When Yankees can't persuade Britishers," remarked the Vice, "they usually proceed to"—

"Pack a High Court of Arbitration," interrupted the Purser.

The quartette straggled through the tall weeds, which prevented farther chaff, and reached the sally port. The heavy gates hung aloft, their duty being discharged by deputy in the shape of long rails resting edgewise in two posts, and with "No Admittance" painted upon a

The British Garrison.

board. The garrison, moving on interior lines, gradually massed itself behind the board, its forefingers taking wary positions within its respective mouths. Behind, and in the centre of the terreplain, towered an enormous haystack. "Behold," said the Purser, "the ingenuity with which the garrison has placed the haystack just where riflemen can take shelter behind it, and command the entrance to the fort, picking off infatuated Yankees who venture upon the drawbridge."

"True," retorted the Cook, "the idea is not unlike that of General Jackson, who used cotton-bales at New Orleans, but I believe it was not Yankees, who were picked off." The contrast between the ideal and the real was so absorbing, as the four stood at the bridge-head, that some time elapsed before they realized that clouds had gathered heavily, and begun to drop their contents.

"My main hatch is open!" shrieked the Vice, as he hurried off to his canoe.

"My tobacco—and it's a rare Brazilian article—is

The Sally Port.

lying in the bottom of my boat!" shouted the Cook, as he followed the Vice.

"The Vice and the Cook will tow up the other boats," ordered the Commodore, "while the Purser and I construct temporary shelter."

Several hundred yards from the fort was a group of trees and a board pile, and to this the commanding officer and the Purser hastened. The trees seemed to have been a favorite resort of cattle, and the contents of the board pile were rotten, but it was not a time to be particular, so a beam was stretched between the limbs of two trees, and boards slanted against it to shed the rain. Fortunately a platform of boards happened to be just where the extempore shed would cover it. When the Vice and the Cook returned, the latter considerately bringing dinner material with him, it was discovered to be noon-day, so the party did justice to bread and butter, cold tongue, and a can of apricots. Suddenly the Vice remarked,

"I suppose these boards beneath our feet are the floor of some late military structure. I can't help noticing how perfectly they are combined for drainage, sagging, as they do, at the centre."

The Commodore had not before noticed the peculiarity alluded to, but now his mathematical eye saw that the depression in the boards was lower than the surface of the surrounding ground. Extracting a trolling line from the Vice's pocket, he lowered a sinker cautiously in a crack between two boards, unrolled considerable line, withdrew it, and remarked,

"I have the pleasure of informing the squadron that during military occupation of the fort, the inmates of the hospital, the ruins of which we behold in front of us, had an abundant supply of cool water from a very deep well, which well is at the present moment directly under us, while the boards which cover it are slowly breaking."

Every one sprang to his feet. While at his home occupation of statesmanship, the Vice never beheld disaster impending over his own party without speedily traversing the whole distance between his own party and the opposition, so on this particular occasion, his instincts impelled him to dash through rain, mud, and thistles toward the ruins of the hospital, whose wall offered the most distinct shelter within view. The Vice wore a helmet, his

The Vampire Bat.

long whiskers fluttered behind him on the breeze, his shoulders and body were covered by a black rubber blanket, his trowsers were rolled high above his stockingless calves, and he wore a huge pair of carpet slippers, which were nearly as wide as they were long. His figure and attitudes, as he ran, were so full of suggestion that the artist preserved them in a series of sketches, severally entitled.

"The Flight of Cain."

"Scotch Laird enjoying His Favorite Weather."

"Study of the Bottom of a Bear's Foot."

"Rip Van Winkle chased by Dogs."

"Mephistophiles Triumphant."

"Election Returns from a Rural District."

"The great Vampire Bat."

The absence of the Vice left his late companions in possession of additional elbow room, but on a rainy day there are blessings more to be desired than elbow room. Among these is a pipe of tobacco, and four walls between which to smoke it. The Cook's precious Brazilian tobacco was wet, the Commodore and the Purser had left their pouches in their boats, but each man had a pipe in his pocket, and it was known that the Vice had in his possession a bag of delicious weed. So dispatches were sent him during a slight lull in the storm, and the Commodore and Purser made a reconnoissance in the direction of the fort. The garrison being invisible, the storming party dashed over the bridge and beneath the temporary portcullis, putting to flight a large body of chickens who were carelessly resting upon their arms in the guard-room. These alarmed the commander of the fort, who at once emerged from headquarters, with an axe upon his shoulder, and himself in dishabille.

The Commodore saluted the commandant, and asked, with due formality, the courtesy of shelter for himself and companions, and for permission to walk about the fort when the rain should cease.

"Is it wantin' to be out av the wet ye are?" asked

the commandant; "come straight into the kitchen an dhry yerselves."

"There are two more of us, yet to come," explained the Commodore.

"Ah, niver ye fear," quoth the old man; "isn't the kitchen in the casemate that held the biggest gun, in the good ould times, an' hasn't a whole company av the Rifles been in there to wanst many's the time."

The casemate proved of generous size, as was also the

The Commandant.

cooking-stove that stood in the midst of it. The commandant's wife and children made haste to place chairs, while one child was detailed to bring in the Vice and the Cook at the double-quick. Soon the quartette sat about the refilled stove, and though the month was July, no one thought to push back his chair. Gradually there stole over the party that delicious drowsiness which is peculiar to a man who has been acting as clothes-horse to a wet suit—a drowsiness

> "That resembles slumber only
> As the mist resembles rain"—

a drowsiness which demands not sleep, but smoke. In short, each member of the expedition was dying for a pipe, but he would have prolonged his sensation of dissolution to its logical end rather than have got out of his chair on the one hand, or, on the other, have ventured to smoke in an apartment which was apparently the host's parlor as well as his kitchen. But the Vice, the Statesman, the moulder of men, came at the critical instant to the rescue of his companions and to that of

> "A nearer one
> Still, and adearer one"—

himself.

"You must find it quite lonesome here at times," he remarked to the commandant of the fort.

"Thrue for yez, an' I do," responded her Majesty's representative.

"Still," continued the Vice, "I suppose you can once in a while take some comfort out of a drop and a smoke?"

The commandant of the fort winked profoundly. The Vice passed his half pint flask stealthily to the custodian of Britain's honor, and the old man, first prudently sending his wife out of the casemate for something, drained the flask with the greatest courtesy and enthusiasm. Then the Vice remarked,

"I suppose you get very good smoking tobacco in Canada, as there is no duty on it, but permit me to leave you a fine pouch of it, as a slight remembrance of your courtesy to us."

The commandant accepted the token of esteem, and smiled his thanks from every line of his wrinkled visage. Then he opened the pouch, and advanced his ancient nose, first cautiously, then critically, and finally with a sniff of decided approbation.

The Commandant's Lady.

"Try it at once," said the Vice, with ill-dissembled eagerness. "Don't hesitate on our account—we are old smokers."

The commandant acted at once upon the suggestion, first courteously passing the bag to his guests. Within three minutes these traditional enemies were smoking the pipe of peace together, nor was lovely woman missing from the circle, for the commandant's lady filled and lit, not exactly a yard, but a "lady-finger" of clay herself, and puffed thereat with great satisfaction.

The rain ended, the party went out to look at the fort, and discovered that what from the outside had appeared a mere earthwork was really a very carefully built fort, with stone quarters, galleries, casemates and revetments, and easy of defence to a mere handful of men.

Just as the party was bidding adieu to their kind entertainers, there occurred an accident which displayed to an unexpected degree the *esprit de corps* of the expedition. The commandant had offered the Commodore some milk for the expedition, if some one would wait an hour for it—the cows were quite a way off, he said. To wait inside a grim fort while the sun shone brightly outside, and four canoes needing inspection on account of damages by rain, was a duty to chill the ardent soul. Just then, however, when the Commodore was wondering if he could safely forget his own morning detail of himself as fleet milkman, and assign this duty to some one else, the commandant's older daughter, heretofore invisible, and of about eighteen or twenty summers, appeared from an adjoining room.

"*I'll* stay, Commodore," shouted three manly voices in unison. The Commodore was so affected by this devotion to the interests of the fleet that he felt shamed into a determination to remain true to his self-appointed duty, but when he beheld the Purser's pleading eyes, more eloquent than any words could be, human sympathy overcame soulless discipline in the Commodore's rugged breast, and the brotherhood of man asserted itself.

The wind and the shower died together, and as each

captain of a vessel had some special reason to wish himself farther on his journey, it was agreed that the squadron should proceed under paddles, and camp for the night at a point which the Vice knew all about, having camped there during a previous cruise with the Alderman. This plan was accepted with expressions of the liveliest satisfaction.

As the Purser rejoined the command with his milk pail, the three Americans were seriously conversing about garrison life, as it exists in the British service.

"I have often read," the Vice was saying, "of the exalted social tone which pervades the British army, and I confess that I am glad to have been admitted even for so short a time into society so select."

"I have always understood," said the Commodore, "that the commandant of an English military post is sure to be a gentleman of high social position at home."

The Cook remarked that "it was pleasant to have the notions of the simple and unaffected manners of the English aristocracy, as derived from contemporaneous literature, so pleasantly confirmed by an actual experience."

"But you know that there isn't any—" put in the Purser.

The Cook went on serenely with his remarks, in the same vein and was so ably seconded by his fellow citizens, that the Purser finally embarked and paddled away, stopping a few yards from shore to shout defiantly back,

"It was all Gladstone's doings, you know. But for

him there would have been a regular garrison there, and may be you wouldn't have been so cordially received."

To be out of doors and at liberty for ten days is, to men without physical vices, wonderfully exhilarating, and enforced confinement by a few hours of rain only intensifies physical spirit and alertness. Every nerve and muscle seems to demand something to do, a mountain to climb, an untamed horse to ride, a locomotive to drive, a regiment to lead into a battle, or—as was the case with the Vice on this particular afternoon—a good, close, vicious political canvass to dash into. To gratify and utilize this sensation, there is no sport superior or equal to that of paddling a canoe. Rowing may lessen the physical disquiet, but while the canoeist sits upright in his boat, voluntarily working only with his arms, and learning of unsupposed physical availability and grace with every motion, the oarsman sways to and fro like the deserted half of a melancholy hinge, which wavers helplessly about in air, always longing for something to attach itself to, but never finding it. Besides, the paddler faces his water and his goal, instead of fixing his eyes unceasingly upon the fleeting past. The oarsman's duties are confined to steady pulling, while with every stroke of his paddle, the canoeist pulls and pushes also, discharging these duties with alternate arms as he works upon the opposite sides of his boat. The exercise is not passive, like that which one takes on horseback, nor does it partake of that mental strain which a man experiences when he takes the helm of his own yacht. It is superior, by far, in physical benefit, to that most exhilarating experience that comes of driving a canoe under full sail and before a brisk breeze. And if, after an hour's work at the beginning of a cruise, the canoeist finds himself the owner of two handfuls of blisters which nobody cares to borrow, he finds himself at its end in possession of a fund of strength, spirits, and clearness of head and heart that are far too precious to lend, although they may have been bought very cheaply.

The paddles used by the modern canoeist are like that represented on the cover of this book. They are very light, being made usually of spruce, an inch and a half in diameter at the largest part of the shaft. For a wide canoe a nine foot paddle is desirable, but for narrower craft one seven and a half feet or even seven feet long is sufficient. A common ferule joint in the middle facilitates close packing. Two joints dividing the paddle in three parts, do not work well in practice. Rubber rings, or the two halves of a three inch rubber ball cut to slip over the shafts prevent the water from dripping inboard.

The squadron had sailed thus far without beholding any of the picturesque which is peculiarly French, but now it hoped that at landing, the essence of Acadia would be visible. It seemed for a few moments as if this hope was about to be realized, for as the boats approached their prospective landing, two quaintly dressed boys stood observantly and quietly upon the bank, instead of dancing and hooting like savages, or casting stones and objurgations at the squadron, as almost any brace of boys in the United States would have done under similar circumstances.

"Note the respectful ways engendered by monarchical institutions," observed the Commodore.

"Rather the absence of the spirit which the heavy hand of despotism has crushed out," replied the Vice.

As the boats were beached, the boys timidly approached them. The Vice, forgetting his first encounter of the picturesque, accosted them in French, and was somewhat confused by their replies until he learned that the youths were of English parentage, and that they lisped.

The boys were soon reinforced by their father, a tall, modest, but self-reliant looking man, who eyed the camping preparations of the party with an interest which was greater than curiosity, and which was explained afterward by the discovery that he had been of the Argonauts of '49.

The Vice, in his capacity of Statesman, knew the honest farmer as a type, only as the principal element of mass-meetings which he sometimes addressed; the Commodore, when in his editorial chair, knew him principally as a subscriber to be secured; the Cook, when playing scribbler, found the farmer-type useful to contrast with other types, and the Purser, when in his studio, knew him only as an occasional adjunct to a pastoral composition.

But after the self-contained, hard-working, rather lonely and diffident farmer had lounged about the camp for a couple of hours that evening, the party learned, as the city-bred man needs sorely to learn about many another farmer, that the old man could see something in a sunset besides tints reducible into pigments, more in a book than its writer's art, that he knew more of the essentials of politics than the editor and statesman combined, and stranger still, that he cared neither to edit a newspaper nor to run for office.

After a good supper and a cheerful pipe or two, the Commodore, who had been extremely quiet for a few moments, announced that he considered it the proper thing for canoeists to sleep in their boats instead of tents.

"Then," said the Commodore, "if the river rises suddenly, you will be in your boat, instead of having it drift away from you."

"And if you turn over in bed, in such case," remarked the Vice, "you'll never know what drowned you."

The Commodore did not reply, for the real object of suggestion was to emphasize one point of superiority of the Red Lake model, after which his own boat and the Cook's were built, over the Chrysalid model affected by the other two mariners. But the Commodore's will was law, and that night the four men slept each in his own canoe, a rubber blanket thrown across a line extending from mast to mast affording protection from dew and possible rain.

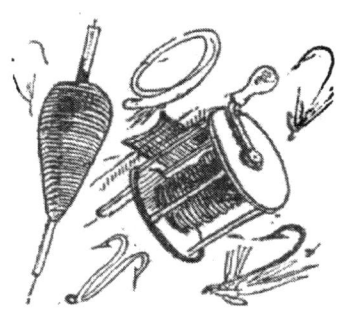

VIII.

THE BEGINNING OF ACADIA.

ON the morning of this day, two canoeists arose from their nautical couches with that satisfied air which betokens a night of peaceful rest, but the Vice and the Purser arose only after many a premonitory groan, and even then they strongly resembled a couple of rough logs from which a single slab had been sawn, so flattened was one side of each. The Commodore eyed them with manifest satisfaction, called the attention of each of them to the appearance of the other, and exclaimed,

"Observe the effect of sleeping in a canoe with ribs and a bottom board! I was curious to see how the experiment would result."

"I wish, then," grunted the Vice, as by vicious pinches he sought to restore animation in his flattened side, "I wish—ow—that your devotion to science had prompted you to try the experiment upon yourself, and borrowed my canoe to do it in."

"Thanks, thanks," rejoined the Commodore, briskly, "but I had an experiment of the same sort to try in my own boat, which has a smooth concave bottom. I beg you will observe how my outlines preserve their habitual shapeliness."

The flat-sided sufferers retired for a bath, and speedily forgot their sorrows. If the morning bath in a city bath-tub is a washer-away of fragments of slumber, and a merry awakener, how much more delightful is the same exercise in an ever-replenishing body of water half a mile wide and hundreds of miles long, enclosed only by blue sky, green trees and brown earth, with no close dining-room and conventional breakfast to be descended to, no morning paper to be read, no vile horse-car to go to business on, nor any hard pavement to tramp over, and no brother man to find fault with, except in that cheerful banter which always comes back to bless the giver. Thus thought the Cook as he stood waist deep in the clear water, and thus he might have continued to think for a long time had his foot not impinged upon the riparian rights of an honest mussel with slightly parted shells.

The Commodore had already been out for provisions, and returned rejoicing.

"Another proof of the superiority of monarchical institutions," said he. "Instead of the prices we have been accustomed to heretofore, I pay twelve cents a-piece for chickens, ten cents per pound for butter, and three cents per dozen for eggs."

"And you are pleased to regard this cheapness as a virtue?" asked the Vice. "Is no one but the buyer to be considered?" How do you suppose people live who sell the products of their industry at such starvation figures? But monarchists and imperialists have but a single idea—to crush the poor."

The Commodore shrunk an inch or two in length and breadth, but soon recovered himself, donned a vicious smile, and announced with assumed cheerfulness that the time had come to "sling the healthy," whereby monarchists, imperialists and republicans would suffer alike.

"What's that?" asked the Cook.

The Commodore grinned sardonically. "He wants to know what, slinging the healthy, is," said he. "Well, he'll know before dinner. It means paddling—paddling in earnest, young man—paddling a ten or fifteen mile stretch, instead of a leisurely half mile."

There seemed no alternative, for the river was as smooth as glass. The sun noted the mirror-like surface of the water, and his natural vanity caused him to rub up his face until its brightness could not be increased. Just by way of refreshing the pleasurable sensation of beholding his face in the water, he dropped his gaze quite frequently upon the blue-shirted backs of the canoeists, until each man imagined that he must have caught some sparks from the camp-fire. Then it seemed as if there must be rain falling from the cloudless sky, for the Cook felt water-drops coursing steadily down his back. The Purser was sure his boat must be leaking, for water was gradually soaking the small canvas cushion on which he sat in the bottom of his canoe. The Vice's slippers grew clammily moist, and the Commodore's eyes filled with water which was not an accumulation of remorseful tears. But no man would debase himself so far as to be the first to cry for mercy.

But the Vice, the Statesman, was true to his profession. To have suggested a rest would have been merely a straight-forward act which even an idiot might have performed. The Vice preferred to gain his point by an exercise of intellect. Half a mile down the stream was a small pier; to this the Vice called the panting Commodore's attention, and exclaimed,

"That, by gosh,* is the identical dock where the Alderman and I went swimming. I assume that all such important precedents are to be respectfully observed?"

"They *are*," said the Commodore, almost fainting with the ecstasy of the transition from despair to hope.

Within ten minutes the boats were beached, and four perspiring canoeists, after an interval of rest, made haste to disrobe and take headers from the pier into the refreshing water.

From this pier the Commodore called the attention of his companions to a glittering spire which shot heavenward a mile down the river, and exclaimed,

"There begins Acadia. Every spire we see hereafter will be of that precise pattern—they are as unchanging as the beautiful faith which our sister Church of Rome maintains."

* The Vice was from an eastern rural district.

The Dock.

"Have we a Ritualist among us?" whispered the Vice to the Cook, with a face full of horror.

"Ye—es," replied the Cook, reluctantly, "but don't think too hardly of the poor fellow. Editors *must* have some sort of religious belief, you know—they're human, like the rest of us—and how can they reconcile their practice to any thing but a religion of mere forms? What would religion be, if it did not provide for every man's own peculiar infirmities?"

The Vice eyed the Commodore with abating horror, nevertheless he began to talk Baptist doctrine to him. He even, to arouse his faculties to the utmost, strode up and down the shore warbling to himself (so the Purser declared) something like this:

> "Baptist, Baptist is my style,
> Baptist born was I.
> I've been baptized in the Baptist way
> And Baptist will I die."

But the Commodore was obdurate, and intimated that the Vice's experience in upsetting from a canoe had something to do with his denominational preference; things had to go according to law in newspaper offices, he said; the newspaper was the highest embodiment of human intellect, and so he reasoned, analogically, that men had no higher model to which to conform religion. The Vice sighed and determined to convert the Commodore—at a more convenient season.

The calm and heat continued, and no one was rude

enough to make suggestions to the Commodore about starting. Indeed, the Purser remembered that he had brought a hammock, which until now he had forgotten. It was one of the most remarkable hammocks in the world—woven of silk by an Italian sailor—wouldn't the Commodore just try it? The Commodore accepted the proffer in gracious spirit; then the Cook remembered that the Commodore had never tried the wonderful, the priceless Brazilian tobacco, and there could be no fitter place than a hammock in which to sample it. The general result was that the Commodore occupied the hammock until the Cook announced dinner, and even then he arose with noticeable reluctance.

After dinner the breeze sprang up again, and as it wafted clouds of dust into the eyes, faces and hair of the expedition, as well as upon their garments, still damp with honest sweat, every one hailed with joy the order to sail. Besides, the dinner had been a mere lunch, and as the largest town on the river was but a few miles distant, the Cook suggested that an excellent dinner might be procured there at a quaint little French inn which he had visited in other days. This suggestion led to a lively race, which as usual in such cases was won by the Cook.* Whether beating or beaten, however, the pleasure of

---

Note by the Cook.—Contradictions of this statement have been received from the Vice and the Purser, but they are couched in language unfit for publication. The proof-sheet of this page has been carefully kept from the eye of the Commodore.

spreading all sails and making the best possible time in a good wind, was more than sufficient reward for all the effort put forth. With a boat fourteen feet long, and weighing, all rigging, spars, personal property, stores, etc., included, a scant hundred and fifty pounds, yet carrying fifty square feet of canvas, the canoeist has to exert to the uttermost his clearness of vision, nicety of touch (at the helm) weather wisdom, and balancing ability. He is himself his own ballast and the principal portion of the cargo. The shifting of five pounds of weight would compel a capsize, and the slightest flaw, carelessly caught, would even more certainly induce the same undesirable result. To keep all dead weight as far as possible below the water line, the navigator sits in the bottom of his boat, his back resting against a small board which, in turn, bears upon the after thwart or bulk-head. In one hand he holds the sheet of his mainsail; if he steers with a rudder, he holds one tiller rope in the same hand, and the other in the remaining digits. If he steers with a paddle, which is for several reasons the preferable mode, he holds the paddle with the hand unoccupied by the sheet; there is thus a steady strain upon both arms, and this strain is also a perfect brace. Some canoeists work the tiller with the feet, and this when properly carried out is a very convenient mode, but not every one who has tried it succeeds in making it work. The time which intervenes between the coming of a flaw and the full fruition of a capsize, is usually about three seconds, but one of these suffices for prevention, if the sailor promptly lets go his sheet or allows his boat's head to go into the wind. In practice, however, a flaw seldom strikes a close-hauled sail; the pilot's ear detects it coming several seconds before it strikes, and so, before it appears, the mainsail is as innocent of the possibility of abetting disaster as if it were the proprietor of a gambling saloon, who had been forewarned by some sympathetic police captain of an impending raid, or a skilful insurance president who knows that the state inspector is coming. How the canoeist's ear detects the coming flaw is the mystery and despair of the novice, though several hours of practice make this wisdom seem an acquisition some centuries old. When the "green" canoeist experiences a flaw, he generally seeks safety by letting go his sheet and at the same time steering "into the wind." Safety is at once assured, but when the boat again takes the "course," the other boats, if sailed by experts, are already too far away to be available if one wishes to borrow an æsthetic idea or a pipe of tobacco. The experienced sailor lets his sheet go sufficiently, but he knows to a breath when the flaw is sufficiently spent to allow him to "haul close" again, and he holds his course to a point all the while, saving some wind by throwing his weight well to windward. If he has a satisfactory family, but lacks as much life insurance as he desires, he will prefer to try a good wind over water not more than five feet deep, (and such water is a hundred times as plentiful as deeper water) but the chance of capsizing a sober canoeist of a week's practice is less than that of falling dead in the street at home; it is as easy to avoid as if it were the risk of stepping over a precipice in full view, for in the former case the catastrophe is as easily foreseen as in the latter. And while the boat is flying (literally, for her bottom barely touches the water, and she can sail at a respectable speed over tide-mud barely glazed with water,) its occupant has every pleasure experienced by the owner of a twenty-thousand dollar yacht. He has the same glorious wind whistling in his ears, the same sharp remonstrance of the waters divided by the bow, the same murmurs of recognition and complaint by the same waters as they reunite under the sternpost, the same sense of triumph over one element, of compulsion of another, which if it had its own way would be only a fitful ally, the same glorious *abandon* of health and spirits revelling in pure air and in endeavor unconstrained by age, sex, or previous conditions of social or business servitude. And when the sail is over, or the season itself is ended, the delightful memories of the cruise are not, as in the case of the yachtsman, palled by recollections of the frightful expense of the crew, or the extortionate charges of ship-builders for repairs. And while the yachtsman lays up his boat for the winter, and bemoans the wasting interest upon her cost, and the various charges for dockage, keeping, etc., the canoeist quietly puts his boat upon his back, or, at worst a cart, carries it to his house, and puts her down in the cellar or

Under the Elms.

up in the garret (after an unsuccessful attempt to have her wintered on top of the piano in the parlor) in either of which places he may visit her as frequently as he pleases, in any weather, and refresh any memories that may seem laggard when recalled.

The party went into camp in the shade of some grand old elms which stood in front of what had once been her Majesty's barracks. During the political changes which had turned the British spear into the Canadian pruning-hook, the barracks had been diverted from their original purpose into homes for the friendless poor; the shore of the river in front of them was, therefore, full of the discarded crockery and broken bottles peculiar to a certain phase of poverty, and as the Vice and the Purser stepped barefooted into the water to carry their boats ashore, the soles of their feet testified to the truth of the scriptural saying "The poor ye have with you always." *

As the expedition landed, weary, foot sore, hungry, unshaven, and covered with the dust of their last camp, the sight of a busy town, full of brisk well-to-do people, caused them to experience to the uttermost the sensations peculiar to the vagabond and the pariah. A marvelously good dinner at a marvelously low price comforted the material part of their inner man, but their mental parts remained ill at ease. So uncomfortable were they that the party

* As boats of the Chrysalid model have prominent keels, and stem-posts that are merely ornamental, they cannot be beached by a gentle tug at the painter, such as is always sufficient with a Red-Lake boat.

took pattern after the vulgar who wish to appear as gentlemen—they purchased and smoked the best cigars in the town. Returned to their camp, the spectacle of a number of well-dressed, sprightly children playing under the trees reminded them strongly of home, where changes of clothing were more numerous than on board canoes, and where whatever bath tub may be available, is not paved with scrap tin and broken glass and crockery.

Suddenly an unexpected, an unhoped for influence appeared upon the scene. A young lady, who apparently had a nephew or niece among the children, strolled toward the water's edge a little way from the boats, and amused herself with the gambols of a huge water-dog. The parlor critic would scarcely have called her beautiful—probably at the Court of Jove there were goddesses more beautiful than Juno, nevertheless Juno ruled men as no rival beauty did. The lady with the dog noticed no member of the expedition, but it was impossible for the mariners to be as unconcerned in return, for maidens who are embodiments of health, strength, grace and modesty are not seen often enough even where maidens most do congregate. The Commodore sat down and leaned against a tree to hide the dusty back of his shirt; the Purser made haste to don a blue jacket which he had fortunately brought with him; the Vice, who, apparently with malice aforethought, had shaved himself, sat in his canoe, adjusted his statesman-like glasses, and took full satisfaction out of the ennobling spectacle, while the Cook, with characteristic modesty, crept within the tent, where he might behold and yet remain invisible. When the lady departed, as unfortunately she did, the quartette debated whether she went on wings, or floated off on one of the clouds that were hovering about, or was wafted away by the fortunate breezes which could express their admiration without being suspected of forwardness or flattery, or, whether she was suddenly translated to a better

The Enchantress.

world, as the Vice enthusiastically declared was no more than her desert. And yet, the material optics of every member of that expedition knew that the lady walked away upon her own feet, as any ordinary mortal would have done, for each of them had gazed industriously after her as long as her form was visible. The difference of opinion led to no dispute, however, for the manners of the expedition had noticeably improved within an hour, and though no canoeist had modified his apparel in any way, each man had something in his face which made him more presentable.

Meanwhile the little clouds which had been previously acting, each for itself, gathered in convention, resolved that in union there was strength, and then proceeded to business. The merry children, with juvenile trust in nature, suspected nothing until they felt it, and then protests were of no avail. But the Commodore took charge of the entire party, and massed it within the expedition's tent, where the children had a glorious time while the navigators strolled about outside and made-believe enjoy the heaven-sent shower-bath. Then the shower departed and so did the children, the shades of night were drawn, and behind these the expedition hid itself while it changed its soaked clothing. Then it lit its evening candle and prepared for bed, the Vice and the Purser insisting that the evening couches should be within the tent instead of the boats. While in the preliminary stages of a discussion, however, a vivacious small dog announced the approach of visitors, and then usnered to the front of the tent a gentleman, a lady and a small hand-wagon. The couple proved to be the parents of one of the children who had been sheltered by the tent during the afternoon, and they had called to express their thanks, some of which were from the tongue and heart, while others were from the hand-wagon, and consisted of bottles of excellent ale, a huge loaf of cake, some dainty preserves, etc. The gentleman proved to be an ex-officer of a famous Canadian regiment, so the Commodore and the Cook talked military affairs with him; he knew all about Dominion politics, so he and the Vice found a point of contact; he was also of English birth, and when the Purser learned this, he monopolized him, and the couple talked church and agriculture, Gladstone and Melton-Mowbray pork pies, while the lady exhibited a degree of tact and vivacity which prevented the other gentlemen from remembering that the place was not a parlor, and that they themselves were not within their respective funereal dress suits. Then several citizens with aquatic tastes dropped in, one by one, and offered various generous hospitalities, and the result of it all was that the expedition thought no more of its shabbiness than if this condition had suddenly gone out of existence.

It was not until an unprecedentedly late hour that the last visitor departed, and the members of the squadron retired with a faint notion that rain was again beginning to patter upon the leaves overhead.

IX.

AREAS OF RAIN.

SLEEP was sedulously courted this morning by the entire squadron, for not only did the late hours and social dissipations of the preceding night have a soporific effect, but a steady rain had set in during the small hours, and not even the Cook felt any disposition to arise and shine. The tent was rather close quarters for four, so the Commodore had slept in his canoe, and for him rising meant stepping out of a dry nest into a steady down-pour. After a while, however, voices began to issue from the tent and a desire for breakfast soon asserted itself. As the camp was in the outskirts of a town, no wood was to be had save through purchase, so the Rob-Roy cuisine was resorted to with eminent success, and a wandering small-boy who spoke nothing but Kanuck of the most rudimentary description, was persuaded to fill an order from the maternal larder.

Breakfast was at last finished, and numerous pipes were smoked to kill time until the rain should cease, but still it poured down with such steady persistency, that it had its effect even upon the buoyant spirits of the quartette. The sole objects of interest which presented themselves were boats laden with hay which drove past the tent-door down the river before the wind. These the Commodore sketched with the adjoining result, and then

Aristocratic.

relapsing into a state of demoralization was maliciously portrayed by the artist on page 147. At length the showers became intermittent, and the two division command

Plebeian.

ers sallied forth in different directions to collate information regarding the rapids.

"One charm of the character of your true rural," remarked the Commodore, on their return to compare notes, "is that he is unconventional. When you have learned the opinions of one, upon matters about him,

The Commodore Weather Bound.

you are not justified in accepting them as those of the community at large."

"Very true," said the Vice. "I have spent two hours in interviewing the honest villagers near the waterside, to ascertain if the rapids, which begin a short half mile below, are passable, and from no two of them did I get the same reply. One said yes, another said no, a third looked doubtful, a fourth encouraging, number five was dumb, and from a dozen or two others I obtained enough of shrugs, gestures, and facial contortions to supply the clown of a pantomime. So little recks your true rural of what doesn't particularly concern him that one fellow, who works in a flour-mill, informed me that there were no rapids whatever, any where in the river."

"Proof positive that he doesn't pay taxes upon property," said the Commodore. "The tax-collector is the grand educator upon local geography: hence, the most intelligent nations of Europe are those which are taxed heaviest."

"The Turks, for instance," suggested the Vice. "I accept your theory, however, for the sake of offering it back to you as proof positive that we Americans are the most intelligent people on the face of the globe."

"The exact bearings of taxation upon the passability of rapids," said the Commodore, "may be clear to a statesman's mind, but the editorial brain fails to record any impression regarding it. The question is, are we to run the rapids or pass around them by canal? I propose first to listen to the counsels of my captains, and then to act according to my own. Officers will speak in reverse order of rank. Cook?"

"Run the rapids by all means," promptly replied the Cook, who had no nautical reputation to lose, but might gain an immense amount without exceeding the demand.

"Purser?" said the Commodore.

The custodian of the fleet's treasure tossed his auburn locks gaily behind his ears, and replied,

"As well ask the bird if it would soar heavenward, the imprisoned soul if it would yearn for light, the poet if he would seek his ideal!"

"Or a duck could he swim," put in the Vice.

"Do you mean that you prefer to run the rapids?" asked the Commodore.

"Certainly," replied the Purser.

"Say so, then," said the Commodore, with editorial sternness, "Vice?"

"The one delight of a canoe cruise," said the Vice, "is to run rapids. I don't know of another joy that compares with it, unless it be that of a Presidential campaign full of personalities."

"I decide in favor of the canal," said the Commodore. "My duty to society demands it. Moreover, I encountered this morning a large number of natives, all of whom without a single exception assured me that the rapids could not be run. Running unknown rapids is attended by considerable danger, and while the loss of a

Statesman, an Artist or a Scribbler might be a blessing to suffering humanity, an Editor cannot be spared. Editors are born, not made, and are consequently very rare."

"Which fact, like that of the crocodile destroying its young," remarked the Vice, "is a proof of the merciful interposition of Providence to save the human race from what might otherwise be a terrible scourge."

As the natives had missed neither spoons, poultry nor any other easily secreted property during the night, they viewed the departing fleet with kindly eyes, and pressed sundry favors upon it. The expedition attempted to advance in column under sail, but it speedily became involved in difficulties with sundry saw-logs and slightly submerged ropes, until all available seamanship was called into exercise to avoid humiliating disaster. When the entrance to the canal was reached, the navigators discovered that the water was spanned, at short intervals, by bridges not only so low as to compel the striking of masts, but also to necessitate the striking of signal staffs fore and aft, and the temporary assumption, by the various commanders, of a physical attitude most truly devout. As the fourth bridge was approached by the expedition, it was also reached by an industrious shower, and no one made haste to pass from under the cover afforded by the structure.

"Think of the poor sailors on the broad ocean, with no bridge to shelter them," remarked the Cook, as he improved the opportunity to light a peaceful pipe. Just then a small stream of water, in search of its final level, meandered between two planks of the bridge, and trickled into the Cook's pipe, producing a sizzle which seemed to greatly titillate the nerves of those who were not smoking. Then another stream struck the helmet of the Vice and broke into what would have been a graceful cascade had not its perfect curve been broken by the official nose. The Purser bowed his head to avoid showing unseemly merriment at the expense of his superior officer, when another stream, heavily charged with the soil which wagons had deposited upon the bridge, insinuated itself between his shirt and his skin. Then began a magnificent but ineffectual struggle of mind against matter. Given, a bridge the planks of which were not more than ten inches wide, and several men whose shoulders exceeded in width any two of the planks, and whose depth of chest, with its environment, also exceeded the distance between any two cracks, and the reader will perceive, more freely than by any logical form of demonstration, the utter futility of free will in a contest against destiny. The best that man can do in such an unequal conflict is to prepare himself as well as possible for the blow, and this the Commodore did by throwing a rubber poncho (a square sheet with a hole in the middle) over his head, the ends dropping outside the gunwales of the boat, and shedding the water into the canal. The wooden decks of the Chrysalids kept water from dripping into the boats except amidships, the oilcloth decking of the flagship served a similar purpose, but the inside of the Cherub was soon deplorable in the extreme.

In time the sun banished the shower, and under its beams the canoeists brightened sufficiently to drop into song, beating time with their paddles. As they approached one bridge, and recurred to the reflection that civilization has its penalties as well as its pleasures, the keeper of the bridge good-naturedly opened it.

"By Jove!" exclaimed the Commodore, "no one but a Frenchman would have been civil enough to do that. Let's sing the 'Marseillaise' for him, and remind him of his far distant home. Now!

> 'Allons, enfants de la patrie.
> Le jour de gloire est arrivè.'"

The song was given with spirit, and with that confidence of accent which song somehow inspires. The squadron, in perfect line, and keeping a rhythmic stroke as of one man, reached the bridge just as they struck the refrain,—

> "Aux armes, citoyens!
> Formez vos battalions!
> Marchez, marchez, qu'un sang impur,
> Abreuve nos sillons."

The bridge-keeper raised himself from the leaning position which he had at first assumed, his eye brightened, a flush of red showed under the dark brown of his cheek.

"That's a magnificent song," he shouted in French. "What do you call it?"

Aux Armes Citoyennes.

Four paddles stopped abruptly in mid-air, four men stared blankly at each other, then the Commodore sank back into his cockpit as nerveless as Salvini in the finale of "La Morte Civile." In a moment he recovered himself enough to gasp,

"True enough; the ancestors of these French Canadians came over a century before Rouget de Lisle was born!"

"What?" exclaimed the Vice, hastily backing out of line and turning his boat, "and that poor fellow knows nothing of the glory of his race, of the rights of man, and things? I'll go back and enlighten him."

"Let him alone," said the Purser. "He knows enough to be polite and sympathetic—to volunteer extra labor that others may be saved annoyance, so he knows more of the rights of man than you can teach him."

The Vice meekly drew back into line, merely asking if it was not nearly dinner-time. As one bank of the canal was heavily covered with weeds, and the other was being frequently traversed by tow-horses, the noon-day meal was taken in the boats, the four being temporarily lashed together that the various viands might be passed back and forth without danger of being dropped overboard. The leisure consequent upon dining enabled the squadron to observe critically the crews of the various barges that passed, and to learn that although the spirit of trade has not altered the French canal-boatmen of Canada from their national model, the environment of circumstance has made the rider of the canal-horse like unto his brother navigators of all climes. The remarks which these gentlemen volunteered as they passed the squadron were all couched in the French tongue, but the accent was that of the Erie canal, the Delaware and Hudson, and all other watery highways upon which the motive power is equine or mulish.

These canalers indeed, as was quickly evident, were of cosmopolitan or at least of republican habit, for so personal did their remarks become that some means of retaliation or self-defence was manifestly necessary. Dignified silence is all very well, but your modern canaler does not appreciate it in the traditional fashion, and when a quiet professional gentleman is invited to "come out of that and have a head put on him" by a burly ruffian, it is apparent that the policy of silence is not always that of wisdom. Under these circumstances it occurred to the Vice, who had been a "Son of Malta," that portions of the extinct ritual might be made available. The Cook was accordingly instructed to hang the expeditionary frying-pan over his forward-thwart and provide himself with a short baton, wherewith to beat it after the manner of a Chinese gong. The next "Bargees" that we encountered opened the usual conversation, inquiring where we were from, and where bound, all which questions were answered with due civility. Then the chaff element cropped out.

"Say, Boss, whar did you get that hat?" The remark was addressed to the Commodore who headed the line. In a resonant voice that officer repeated: "He asks where did I get my hat."

Then the Vice, "He asks where did he get his hat?"

Then the Purser, "He asks where did he get his hat?"

Then the Cook, "He asks where did he get his hat?" and then lifting his bâton he proclaimed in a stentorian voice RECORDED! and mightily smote the frying-pan till it rung again. The invariable sequence of this was a momentary pause, during which the squadron usually passed out of ear-shot. Sometimes however, the canalers attempted a continuation of the attack, as for instance:

"Now then," (but really this part of the sentence can only be represented by blanks) "Come out o' that, and I'll learn yer."

Commodore. "He calls us scions of a noble race."

Vice. "He calls us scions of a noble race."

Purser. "He calls us scions of a noble race."

Cook. "He calls us scions of a noble race. Recorded! WHANG!!"

"The recorded answer turneth away chaff," said the Vice somewhat irreverently after the success of the experiment was established, and so it was, for the profane resources of the most fluent mule-driver failed him in the presence of the frying-pan.

Soon after dinner the squadron approached a lock, and the Commodore went ashore to exhibit the passes of his command. As the collective measurement of the boats did not reach ten tons, the four had been included in a single pass, the cost of which was twenty cents, and this sufficed for the dozen locks which were to be passed before the smooth water of the river could again be reached. It was probably a realization of the small amount of money which their labor represented which made the various lock-keepers so solemn of mien as they labored over their gates to let the Liliputian squadron through. The walls of each lock were substantially built of huge blocks of grey stone, and as the water subsided rapidly the Artist imagined himself being let down into a dark dungeon. He hastily drew his portfolio from a locker, and proceeded to sketch a study for a "Prisoner of Chillon," hugging the shady side of the lock as he did so. The sketch proceeded to his satisfaction, and then some loose earth behind the stones ejected through a crack some of its superfluous moisture in a parabolic curve over the Artist's shoulder, and upon the sketch, putting in some half tints which gave the picture an air of extreme realism and antiquity.

Reaching at length a long stretch of canal upon which no boats were visible, the squadron disembarked and washed its respective faces with soap, an operation rendered necessary by the drippings it had encountered under the bridge, and during the various showers. An hour later, the face of the Vice looked as if it had been liberally but carelessly patched with court-plaster. Fragments of skin fluttered aimlessly from his cheeks and brow, while his Roman nose was as picturesque as the brown shoulders of a tramp who had lately begged a very ragged white shirt. The Vice became conscious that he was attracting attention, and a pocket-mirror, furtively consulted, revealed to him the cause. He passed his mirror to the others, and the merriment of the party came to a sudden stop, for every one else was displaying symptoms of impending trouble of the same sort. Not one of them had experienced an hour of sunshine a day for months; their faces had been burning steadily for days, and the alkali of the soap had destroyed the last bond between the burned cuticle and that beneath. The Purser suggested that cold cream, being peculiarly a French production, could doubtless be found in the next village, but the Vice said him nay.

"Frenchmen who don't know the Marseillaise when they hear it," said he, "can't be expected to know anything about the appliances of modern civilization."

The morning's rain, the late start and sundry delays had hindered the fleet more than it realized, and the sun was setting before the canal was half-way passed. It became necessary therefore to camp on the canal bank, but this was no great hardship, as a smooth strip of green sward opportunely presented itself on the side away from the tow-path, as shown at the left of this sketch. A moral title is appended to this illustration because the Vice went off by himself after supplies and came back thoroughly sobered, as he intimated, by the sublime

Alone with his Conscience.

immensity of the canal, which, he said, stretched away before him like the narrow path which he remembered as depicted in the "Pilgrim's Progress" of his boyhood.

Indeed there was a pastoral beauty about this canal which one is not apt to associate with artificial waterways. It was but a few miles in length and skirted a lovely valley, rich in historic association and beautifully diversified by wood and meadow, hill and stream. Beyond the lowlands, as shown in the sketch, rose a commanding and somewhat isolated mountain range which caught the last rays of the setting sun, and welcomed him again in the morning in such charming fashion that it was simple luxury to exist within the range of its influence. Since crossing the line, too, minor incidents of daily recurrence recalled the fact that this valley was first penetrated by emissaries of "Mother Church." On every side the little tin covered spires, one just like the other, arose, and at sunrise and sunset, the matin and vesper bells sent their notes far and near, reminding all within range that the priest was at the altar holding aloft the sacred emblems and repeating the angelus. The members of the expedition were all Protestants by birth and association, but there was not one of them who had not a tender spot in his heart when the bells rang out and he knew that hundreds of fellow beings, far and near, paused a moment at their tasks to repeat the prayer that the church had taught them to say. These little churches, of which this may serve as a type, form a charming feature of the Acadian land. You may walk into any of them at any hour, and some are very quaint, and in a strange fashion touching, in their interior design and adornment. It seemed as though the prayers of generations of simple minded folk were imprisoned there, willing and ever anxious to get up to heaven, if that were possible, and

The Typical Church.

yet hampered somehow so that they did not make it out. Often as one or another of the quartette strolled into a village church and sat down in the suggestive silence, a man or woman would come in and kneeling repeat a prayer. To say that the act is mechanical and heartless is not to the purpose. It may be both mechanical and heartless, but it is not meaningless, and through it and other like observances, the church retains a tolerably stronghold upon a very considerable fraction of Christendom. Would that the home-feeling could be as successfully cultivated by some of our Protestant sects as it seems to be by the church of Rome. Perhaps however the home feeling as it there exists is incompatible with advanced thought, and the liquefaction of gases, and Boston Monday Lectures.

So at least the Vice was remarking when he suddenly became aware that a canal-propeller was coming down his recent straight and narrow path, towing behind her an endless chain of lumber barges. Anxiety for the boats banished every other sentiment. The Red Lakers were confidently trusted to take care of themselves by their commanders, but Chrysalids must be carefully tended and held off shore, lest the swell should dash them against the stone facing of the embankment. Considering what the Rochefort had been through on her various lee shores, this solicitude seemed rather superfluous. Furthermore, no perceptible swell was caused by the passage of the tow, and the only notable result was that the Purser, in his anxiety to hold the Arethusela off shore with a boat-hook, lost his balance and took a ducking, much to the amusement of spectators on the canal boats.

An exquisite moonlit night was this on the canal. The tent stood white against the grassy bank, the canal glittered, from far away could be heard the hoarse roar of rapids, and farther still the blue mountain range rose flat against the sky as if it had no irregularities save those which marked its outline. Only one anxiety marred the serenity of the fleet.

Ever since "the Enchantress" arose upon its horizon, one member of the command who shall be nameless, had not been quite in his right mind. While passing along the canal, he had evinced a preference for such airs as "Annie Laurie" and "The Girl I left behind Me," while the "Mulligan Guards" and the Marseillaise failed to stir his soul as was their wont. This evening he passed walking up and down the canal bank in the moonlight, apart from the rest, and he was even suspected of declaiming poetry *sotto-voce*. There the squadron left him when it turned in.

After a long interval of quiet, no one knows what the hour was, the sleepers were softly awakened by the enthusiast, who by the straggling moonbeams was seen with a finger on his lips as an injunction of silence, while with the other hand he pointed toward the remains of the camp-fire in front of the tent. Each man arose noiselessly; one softly cocked his revolver, another grasped a boat hook, while a third clutched two empty beer-bottles, stole out of the tent, and peered warily about, in the shadows of the trees. Each man saw that the boats were safe, and as all cargoes had been removed to the tent before nightfall, the nature of the danger which impended could not be imagined by any one. The demented man threw several twigs upon the smouldering embers, thus making a bright light; then he squatted near the fire, motioned to the others to take similar attitudes, and spoke thus to his mystified auditors:

"Gentlemen, for years I have endeavored to formulate a definition of the phrase 'pretty girl;' not to give a mere literal description, but one which should be artistic as well as truthful, and have the virtue, peculiar to all true art, of suggesting more than it says. At last I have fully succeeded; or, rather, a glorious inspiration has enlightened me. Before disclosing this marvel of truth and poetry, I beg you to give me your own definitions of the same precious phrase—they will be useful by way of contrast."

"I can better tell you what a pretty girl is *not*," answered one of the party promptly. "She is not an imbecile who rouses people at dead of night for the idiotic purpose of revising standard lexicography."

"Nor is she," quoth another, who, being a very light sleeper, sprang to his feet, in a violent fit of trembling, on being aroused, "nor is she a being who will in cold blood frighten an honest fellow almost to death."

"Nor a person whose literary musings disturb the slumber of any one, unless, haply, he be editor of a paper containing a poet's column," said the third.

"Listen, then," replied the lunatic, his look of scorn giving place to a lambent light from within, which irradiated his pale features. "A pretty girl is a person from whose glass you are willing to drink, after she is done with it."

For several moments there was dead silence, then somebody asked in the iciest of tones,

"And you aroused us only for the purpose of imparting this."

"I did."

"Have I offered you a single affront since the cruise began?" asked another. "I certainly have tried hard to do my duty, and have never discriminated knowingly against any one."

"You are guiltless," was the reply.

"I suppose I am the guilty one," groaned the third. "I gave him a cigar to-day which was not what it should have been. But how out of all proportion to the offence is the punishment!"

The object of these denunciations, remaining unchanged of mien, began again to pace the bank beneath the moon-beams, while his companions returned to their blankets and failed miserably to devise any vengeance commensurate with his shameful act.

At length the wisest of the trio, raising himself on his elbow, exclaimed "I have it—make him marry one."

X.

ACADIA.

AT length the voyagers seemed really in Acadia. A large village at the lower end of the canal exhibited in charming profusion the red-tiled roofs, white stuccoed cottages, and verandahs peculiar to French village architecture; all signs over the shop-doors were in French, and nearly all of them indicated that spirituous liquors were sold there; the native stare was of short duration and respectful, instead of long drawn and insolent, as it would have been at any canal terminus in the United States, and the village dogs did not respond to whistles delivered in the American manner. A single new house with Mansard roof had intruded itself in the village, but the Cook promptly suggested that it must belong to some fugitive American statesman, so it could not be considered as part of the village proper.

At this suggestion the Vice became pensive and was presently discovered questioning a resident as to the personal appearance of certain American sojourners. His curiosity was pardonable as he had been conspicuous in breaking up a famous metropolitan Ring, and knew personally some of its fugitive fragments.

No factory reared its horrid front aloft, so the village maidens were meek-eyed and healthy, and the young men did not congregate at street corners with hands in pockets. Two or three score of men stood upon the walls of the final lock, to look at the boats, but they displayed none of the officious curiosity which any able-bodied American citizen would have considered necessary under like circumstances. To the Commodore, the Purser and the Cook the change from the restless activity with which they were familiar was inexpressibly delightful, but the Vice regarded everything with cold suspicion.

"The natural result of monarchical rule," was his incessant comment upon whatever he saw. "There is water-power enough going to waste," said he, pointing to the rapids, "for a manufacturing city such as the world has never seen. Capital would be attracted, labor would follow, facilities for navigation would increase, farmers would have a home market for their produce, real estate would increase in value, and local politics would become a science. But see it as it is! Why, I doubt if it has a board of aldermen, or even a mayor!"

"Then it is Acadia indeed," murmured the Purser, raising his head from a sketch he had hastily made of a sweet-faced girl who was gazing wonderingly yet modestly from a window.

From the river below the lock the expedition saw the foot of the rapids, and near them a ruined fort. A double invitation to view the picturesque was not to be

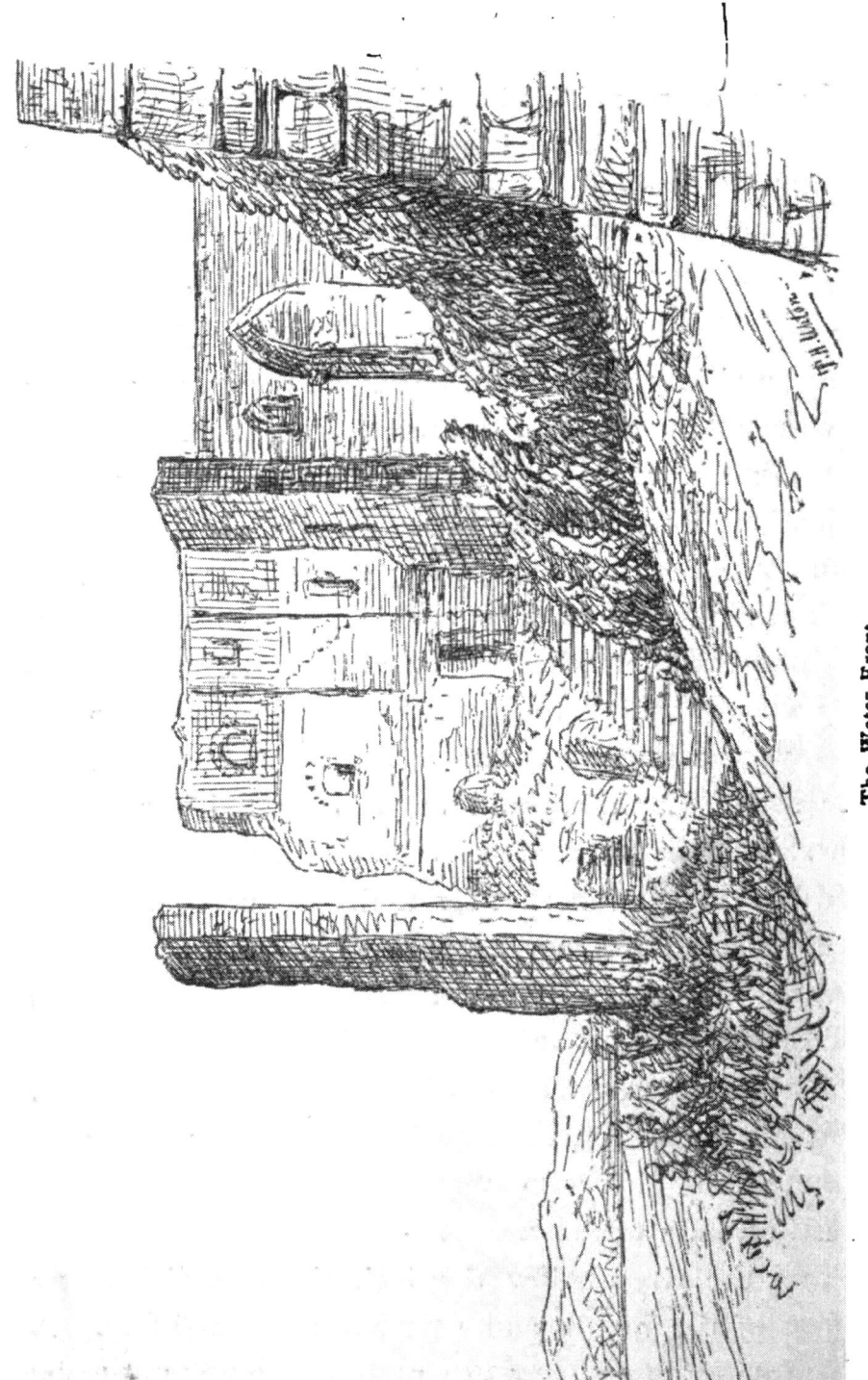

The Water Front.

declined, so every one paddled up as far as the rapids would allow. The fort bore date of 1711, and tradition said that it had been constructed for defence against the Indians, in the days when Canada was still New France, from which it was safe to infer that the North American savage was not in the habit of rounding rapids by canal when he disported himself in his light canoe. The work had been stripped to its bare walls, not by relic-hunters but by searchers after seasoned fuel, and its water-wall had fallen in, but enough remained to show the plan of the work. The Commodore and the Purser broiled in the sun at the gateless sally-port and endeavored to reconstruct the work in the interest of romance. They filled it with picturesque men-at-arms, gallant officers, and venerable priests, and took care not to omit the occasional Indian maiden, while the Vice calculated the cost of transforming the work into a distillery, and the Cook, who had climbed to a sealed loophole overhead in search of reflections which did not appear, gently led the thoughts of the romancers back to the real by an occasional shower of partly pulverized mortar.

It presently occurred to him, however, that the stock of bread was running low, only one loaf being left from the supply laid in beyond the line. He accordingly made a requisition on the Purser for the necessary funds and paddled off to the village. In a few moments he was seen returning, partly concealed behind something which he had placed on the forward deck. As the bow touched

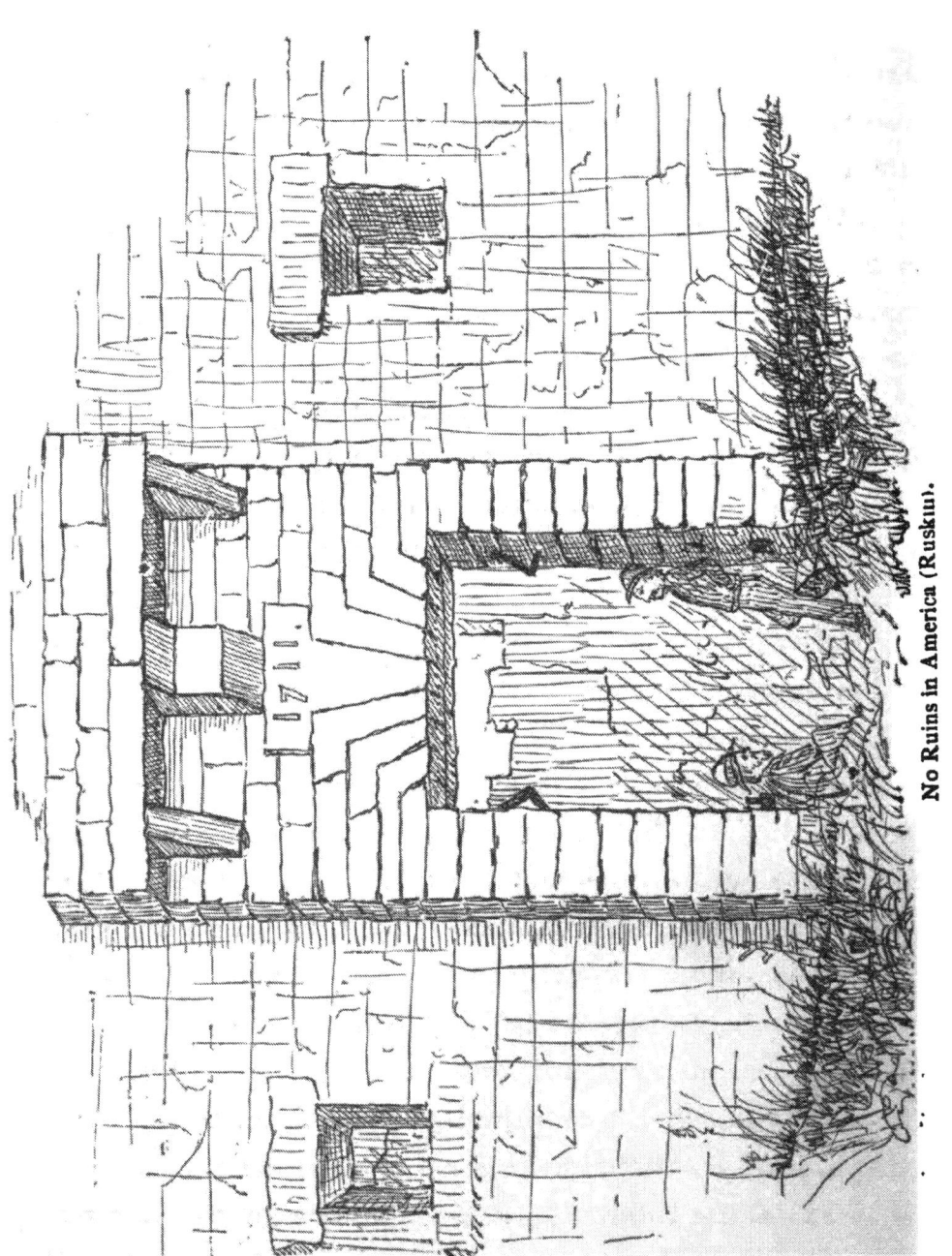

No Ruins in America (Ruskin).

the sand the mysterious object was seen to be merely a loaf of bread beside which, for the sake of contrast, the Cook had laid the remaining loaf of the United States pattern.

The Vice regarded the two with a puzzled air. "Why," he asked, "should forty millions of people living in a free republic, be content with loaves of such diminutive size

Two Loaves—a Contrast.

when the subjects of a despotic monarchy are provided with bread on a scale so truly magnificent?"

"The loaves are to one another in an inverse proportion to the population which they represent," said the Cook.

In quality and price, this loaf compares favorably with that of the American baker, but in size and shape it is unlike anything that elsewhere exists under the same name. Its shape is that of a cloven mountain, and its size—well, if such loaves were used in Judea eighteen hundred years ago, the miracle of the feeding of the five thousand would not seem so very wonderful after all. A single loaf materially increased the draft of the Cook's boat, and had he bought four, as he had expected to do, it would have been necessary to have chartered a store-ship.

As the party sat in the shadow of one of the water bastions and viewed the rapids in their changing forms but changeless beauty, the Vice fell into gloomy reverie.

"It's always so," said he. "We've paddled through a straight cut canal for ten miles, been drenched with water and wind, jeered by mule-drivers, and in French, too,—loosened the skin from our faces, caused heaven only knows how much inward profanity among lock-keepers, lost a whole day and ten miles of scenery, and all because we were afraid to run the rapids, which would have brought us here in an hour. It's the same way in politics; caution means labor and trouble, but if you dash ahead in spite of every thing and every body, you're sure to come out all right. The Alderman always said—"

"It isn't too late yet," interrupted the Commodore. "I am so desirous of seeing some one run those rapids that I will be one of any two to carry your boat as far up the stream as you like, if you will run down in her."

"Agreed!" shouted the Vice, "but—" here he prudently admitted to himself the defects of the model of *his* boat, "I wonder if the Cook wouldn't rather do it in the Cherub—you will find it far the easier to carry."

"Certainly," replied the Cook; "besides, she is far safer, faster and more manageable than your craft. She has no keel to catch upon a rock and tip one over, and her peculiar construction makes it impossible to start a leak, no matter how hard you may strike a stone with her."

The Cherub was promptly unloaded and carried up the stream half a mile, when the Cook seeing an almost unbroken line of rocks crossing the river, stopped her bearers. He then divested himself of all clothing except such as is technically denominated "gents underwear." The boat was placed in the water, heading up stream, and the Cook embarked, bracing his back against the amidship thwart, and his knees against the sides. The painter was thrown in, and he started to paddle out into the stream, but the current was in the habit of working its own sweet will upon floating bodies, and it promptly signified as much to the Cook by whirling him around so rapidly that the force of rotary motion almost deprived him of his scalp and whiskers—his helmet he had thoughtfully left ashore. Then the boat danced merrily along, saluting each inviting rock with a long soft caress, yet obeying the paddle with an alacrity of which no Chrysalid canoe could ever be capable. The time occupied by the trip seemed so great to the Cook, that a thousand years added or subtracted would have had no perceptible influence upon the total; according to the Commodore's pulse, however, (all watches having stopped) rather less than four minutes had elapsed since the start when the Cook paddled the Cherub up to the smooth beach below the rapid, and found that she had not shipped a drop of water, nor started, in striking the rocks, anything more important than varnish.

The four sat for a while longer under the shadow of

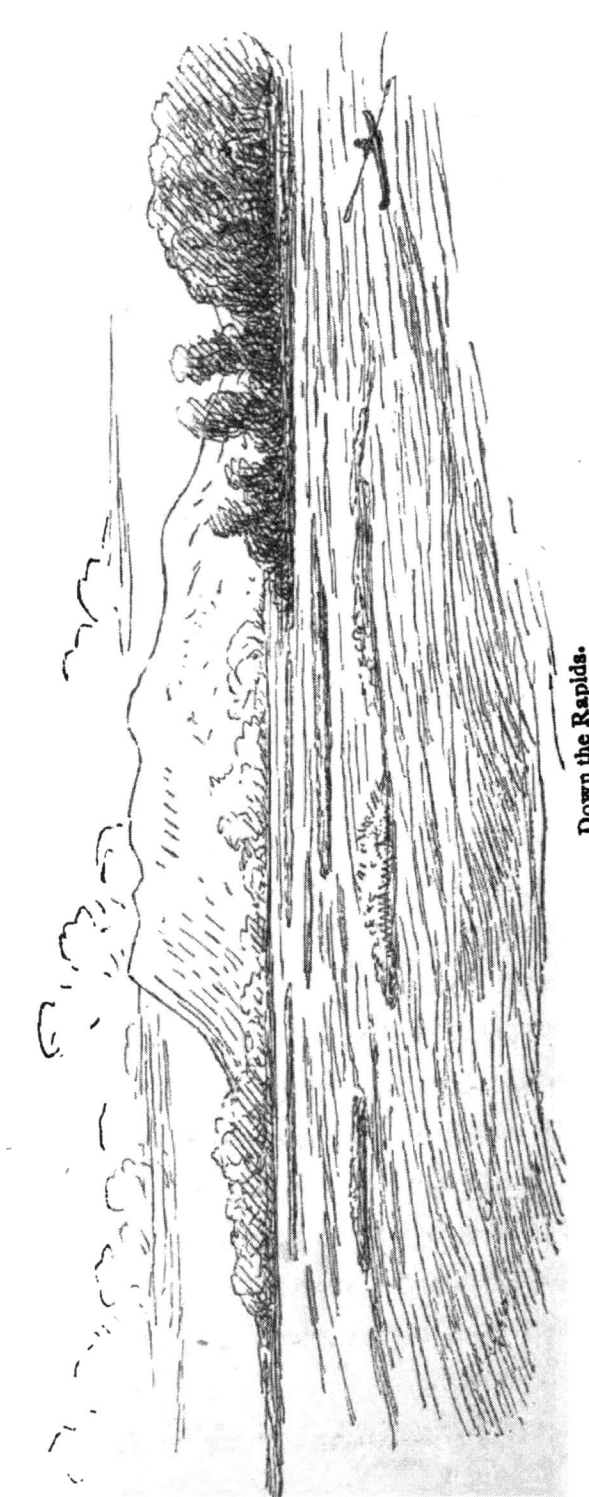
Down the Rapids.

A HIGH TEMPERATURE.

the main gateway, and then proceeded on their way in order to reach a camping ground not in the immediate vicinity of any village.

Upon the broad basin into which the river spread below the fort, the sun shone with a fierceness which set at naught the vulgar theory that solar heat decreases as one goes northward. The voyagers decided, without a dissenting voice, that the isothermal line which reached this portion of Canada was that of the Desert of Sahara, and the Vice, whose scientific ideas were rather vague, suggested that it had probably passed through several blast-furnaces and a ratification meeting on its way north. A gentle breeze finally came to the relief of the party, and at the same time there came certain of the natives to inquire about the speed, etc., of the boats, and as the river at this point was very wide, and the canoeists were not averse to displaying their seamanship, the boats were soon doing the picturesque to the delight of all beholders. Suddenly, however, the breeze took offence at something and vanished, leaving the boats a mile or two from shore. Paddles were manfully plied, the nearest shade upon the banks being several miles away. As no one but a denizen of the abode of the finally impenitent could realize what the heat of that afternoon actually was, it is extremely unlikely that the tale will ever be told, but the Purser solemnly declares unto this day that the sleeve of his blue flannel shirt was scorched by the sun.

The fresh meat purchased at the end of the canal

having succumbed to the heat, the expedition went out in a body, on making camp, in search of animal food. The nearest house seemed miles away, so the Vice took to his favorite pastime of trolling for pickerel, the Purser went into the forest with the Vice's gun, and the Commodore and the Cook started, with boat-hooks, to secure bullfrogs for a fricassee. The Vice caught nothing, as men universally do when they troll, the Purser got nothing but a bruised shoulder, while the Commodore and the Cook, having failed to secure so much as a single batrachian, lost what little character they had for perseverance under difficulties, and swore roundly that the French inhabitants had hunted the frogs till they were too shy to be successfully harpooned. The voyagers fell back upon their canned provisions, made a tolerably satisfactory supper and straightway engaged in a discussion on the kinds of wood available in that most important branch of industry, the construction of canoes, and their accessories.

American white-cedar, they concluded, is undoubtedly the best of all woods for building light boats. It is now exported for this purpose to all parts of the world where artistic boat-building is practiced. Its structure is such that a blow or scrape, such as boats are likely to receive, merely indents without splintering or splitting. It is moreover very light. It has no special beauty of grain but takes varnish well and has an agreeable color, which improves with age.

A Quiet Cove.

Oak is handsomer in appearance, but is too heavy and splinters badly at the edges when exposed to wear and tear. It is usually the best available wood for keels and timbers.

Spanish cedar splits too easily to be used for planking, but makes a handsome deck, and is strong enough when properly supported by carlines.

Butternut is a little heavier than cedar, but is somewhat harder and tougher, and is far more beautiful in color and grain. In point of texture and toughness there is small choice between the two. If one is willing to paddle a pound or two of additional weight for the sake of appearances, let him choose butternut. If not, white cedar is best. Clear butternut can be had in longer and wider strips than cedar.

For stem and stern posts hackmatack is given the preference, by nearly all builders. For the timbers, carlines, and interior braces of all sorts, tough, non-splitable woods are used, different builders having different favorites.

The masts technically denominated the "main" and "dandy," may be of white-ash, spruce or pine—the last being lightest and weakest. They should be carried up without any taper, a short distance above the deck—say three feet for the main and two for the dandy. This is not very essential, it merely makes them bend more symmetrically under sail pressure. Ash is heavier than spruce, but more slender and graceful spars may be made from it, owing to its greater strength. The Commodore having tried both, rather prefers ash. Some members of the New York Club have used bamboo for masts with satisfactory results; for its weight it is certainly the strongest of spars, and in appearance it is all that can be desired, except that it does not taper quite enough at the top to suit a fastidious eye. This objection might be overcome by using a topmast of pine or spruce.

It is almost always convenient to have the masts of a canoe jointed, so that they can be readily stowed below decks. The simplest and cheapest way is to place the mast so that it shall be an inch and a quarter or less at the joint, that being the largest regular size of fishing-rod ferrules. Such joints have been fully tested and are strong enough. The device known as the "sliding gunter" is a brass fitting which holds the main topmast and slides up and down the mainmast, operated by a halyard. It works very well when in perfect order, but is apt to give trouble when the parts get wet. Moreover it necessitates a clumsily large lower-mast, since this part must be deeply grooved to receive the topmast-halyard *over* which the "gunter" slides. The Vice who has tried the sliding gunter rig has decided to adopt a simple nine-foot mast with a mainsail like that shown in the illustration on page 107, and a ferrule joint. The sail runs up and down on rings as do those of the Red Lakers, and having throat and peak halyards attached to the gaff, the peak can be dropped or raised without lowering the sail. This has the effect of reefing and shaking out without the bother of tying the reef-points shown in the sketch referred to, on the lower part of the mainsail.

The Red Lakers, by the way, are reefed by means of a small brass S. hook carried at the peak of each sail. The sail is lowered away and this hook passed through any one of the rings on which it runs. When hoisted again the sail is of course correspondingly reduced in area.

It was ten o'clock before the squadron had settled all this and was content to turn in.

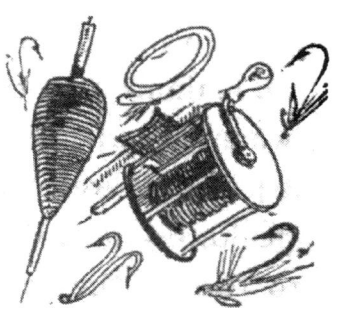

XI.

SEVERAL OTHER DAYS.

THE disgust of the voyagers on the next morning, when they found themselves reduced to breakfasting on bread and coffee, was provocative of vigorous paddling, and a large town was soon reached. The voyagers passed en route a small Indian camp, in which were exhibited some of the positive results of civilized environment, for one of the men had a beard, and the only visible squaw wore an apron with pockets. As the town was one at which the expedition expected many letters, there was a movement in force upon the post-office, which consisted of two cigar boxes upon the table of a sitting-room; one of these contained letters received, and the other mail matter to be transmitted; one contained, after the expedition had received its letters, a single postal card, and the other, when the voyagers deposited their home and business correspondence, was so full that the pleasant lady in charge was visibly affected by the sudden increase of business. There were several streets of very old and very quaint cottages, and a church, externally a duplicate of every other church on the river, and containing an odd yet touching assortment of votive offerings. Among these was a huge model of a full-rigged ship; this swung aloft from the centre of the ceiling, and doubtless kept nervous worshippers from the pews directly beneath it. The value of such an object of contemplation must be inestimable for the adolescent portion of the congregation, that is if the Acadian fancy is as much given over to dreams of piratical adventure on the high seas, as is that of American youth.

Three women were upon their knees in the church; two were utterly oblivious to the entrance of the outlandish foreign quartette, but the third kept alive the faith of man in womanish curiosity, for she stared at the party as long as it was visible. The four sailors walked around the side aisles past the " Stations of the Cross," more, it must be admitted, from longings artistic rather than devout, and were about to leave the church, when two bright looking youths of seventeen or eighteen entered the organ loft, and sang several hymns, accompanying themselves with the organ which was presumably blown by a third. The Vice interviewed them and asked what portion of the service they had been conducting, and learned that they had been singing merely for amusement. Fancy two healthy young Americans going into church during business hours, and singing hymns for purposes of personal diversion! Their associates would promptly cut their acquaintance, their employers would discharge them for laziness, and their parents, if truly affectionate, would hasten to call a physician skilled in treating the victims of mental aberration. The quartette concluded that their fond imaginings regarding the uses of aerial ships had been at fault. Maritime adventure can have no place in the Acadian mind.

A careful survey of the picturesque little hamlet showed that it was infested, though not infected, by a railroad; from this the whole village shrunk away, so that a modern "Railway Hotel," which stood near the station, stood alone, in unrelieved ugliness. The Vice, with his prejudice against every thing foreign, insisted upon the expedition dining at this hotel, because it reminded him of home, and within half an hour he endured the worst meal that had ever been set before him. The Cook, who had been detailed to watch the boats while his associates dined, sank into a peaceful slumber in the Cherub, and became an object of interest to several natives and many hundreds of flies. The former, though somewhat curious, were too polite to arouse the sleeping watchman, but the latter being evidently summer visitors from the States, had neither conscience nor modesty, so the slumberer awoke and devoted some moments to drowsy sympathy for the defunct Pharaoh and his people who suffered under the seventh plague. Then he paced the river-bank, looking about for the picturesque, and was rewarded by a glimpse of the old, old story, which went down the river road between a bashful young man and a comely maiden.

Near this point the river contained several beautiful

islands, and to one of these the squadron made its way after dinner. The distance was small—a mere matter of five miles—but the fact that it had to be traversed by paddle and under a blazing sun, caused the trip to seem fully long enough for an afternoon voyage. A delightful camping ground was finally reached, however; a narrow grassy plateau spreading itself under a belt of thick trees, with lovely outlooks up and down the river. It was the Commodore's tour of duty for forage, and after a lesson in Canadian French from the Vice, who had it at second hand from the Alderman, he paddled over to the mainland. The substance of his instructions was that milk instead of being "lait" was "lât," sounding the final "T," also that the final "S" was in most cases sounded. He tried the nearest house.

"Bon jour, Madame. Avez vous du lât, à vendre?" Glances exchanged among the members of the household with frequent repetitions of the word "lât."

"Comment, M'sieu?"

The Commodore repeated the sentence. Same effect.

"Ne comprens pas."

Another trial with some changes of structure and pronunciation.

"M'sieu, we no speak Anglais."

The Commodore went his way to the next house, half a mile distant, and protected by a black dog of great apparent enterprise. Interview substantially duplicated.

At the third house the discovery was made that the

Alderman's information as to the pronunciation of "lait" was erroneous.

Pronouncing the word in usual manner he was readily understood, but there was no milk to be had. So he paddled over to the island again and approached the somewhat "swell" mansion of the proprietor, which had been shunned in the first instance because the occupants of such mansions not infrequently scorn the advances of canoeists in the direction of supplies. Ascending a foot-path from the landing, the Commodore found himself before a square brick house standing in the midst of forest trees, many being superb specimens of spruce and balsam, which sent their perfect spires of green sixty or seventy feet upward. The underbrush had been cleared away, so that a somewhat broken lawn spread from the house to the edge of the bluff, and through the tree-trunks there opened an expanse of rich meadow-land dotted with cottages crossed by lines of dark coniferous woods, and backed by the blue Belœil range. Lost in the contemplation of the delicious landscape, the Commodore was for a time merged in the love of nature, but a rude interruption was in store for him. No sign of human life had been visible when he turned his back upon the house and became absorbed in the contemplation of the beautiful, but a sudden bark rang upon the air and was instantly taken up, as it seemed from all parts of the island. The case of James Fitzjames and the ambuscaded Highlanders flashed through his mind as a parallel one:

A Charming Landscape.

> "Instant through copse and heath arose
> Bonnets and spears and bended bows."

He turned from the scene which the Artist has depicted and beheld what is shown on the following page. The apparent relative dimensions of himself and the dogs are faithfully preserved.

On they came, but by this time the Commodorial soul had returned from its æsthetic wanderings. If there is one thing of which he is less afraid than another, it is dogs. Consequently when the leader, a shaggy brute of great external ferocity, reached him, he remarked in a low tone of voice, "One moment, old chap. You are making a great mistake. It is all right. I am going to the house for milk." "Major," for that turned out to be his name, accepted the explanation with perfect courtesy, told his followers that it wasn't the fellow he thought, and would they hush their noise, and so all fared along together with occasional growls from still suspicious members of the cortége, and turned the corner of the house, where were seen two seemly maidens of the peasant class, sitting on a verandah with their needle-work.

"Bon jour, Mesdemoiselles," said the Commodore, raising his helmet. "Nous sommes campé la-bas, et nous avons besoin de lait, de pain et de beurre." The last few words had a reassuring Olendorfesque sound, which, as it were, set the speaker on his pins.

The girls looked at one another doubtfully, "Il parle Allemand, n'est ce pas, Louise?" said one.

A Shock to the Commodore's Nerves.

"Mais non," said the other, "Je crois que c'est l'Anglais."

The Commodore seated himself on the steps and buried his head in his hands. One of the dogs whined and poked a cold, sympathetic nose against his cheek. It presently occurred to him that the silence, which was becoming embarrassing, was in danger of being broken by the irrepressible laughter of the young women, who continued their work with mischievous glances at their discomfited visitor. The Commodore is a bashful man, and it has always seemed to him that the laughter of girls is particularly and peculiarly derisive. However, by dint of frequent repetitions of "pain" "beurre" and "lait," he at length succeeded in making himself understood.

The two girls bestirred themselves to procure the desired articles, which by the way proved to be of excellent quality and of absurdly low price. Meanwhile the dogs had become so friendly as to be troublesome, and the two biggest were actually fighting for the privilege of receiving personal attention.

On hearing of this experience, the Purser, who is very fond of dogs, was anxious to be detailed for milk at once, and the Vice, who is,

> "Steel amid the din of arms
> And wax amid the fair,"

longed to air his French in connection with the girls, whom the Commodore represented as possessed of rare charms and engaging manners. It was evident that there would be no trouble about the milk detail at this camp. Indeed a rivalry sprang up between the Purser and the Vice which was only kept within bounds by the necessity of a co-partnership, one being as hopelessly embarrassed in canine society as was the other in that of young women. It followed as a natural result that they invariably went for milk in company and were a long time in getting it. The Vice's French was cultivated to a degree which left him without a rival in the fleet, while the two always came back to camp with a retinue of dogs which nearly drove the Cook crazy by investigating the expeditionary stores.

On the grassy plateau before mentioned, the four graceful boats lay side by side, and in them as the fire burned low, the four voyagers composed themselves to rest, and the Cook and Purser were lulled to slumber by the tones of the Vice who pointed out the constellations, and discoursed learnedly of the precession of the equinoxes. The Commodore, who chanced to be somewhat wakeful, feigned an interest in astronomy, which he had never before displayed, and evinced such an appetite for sidereal nomenclature that he presently had the Vice out of bed, so to speak, and shiveringly endeavoring to discover certain hypothetical stars whose locality the Commodore carefully described, but which could not be seen from the recumbent position occupied by his companion. Having for a sufficient space indulged in this justifiable revenge for certain insubordinate acts on the part of the

Vice, the Commodore suddenly became sleepy, and left the astronomer to discover the ruse at his leisure.

The next day was Sunday and sunny, and a canvass of commanders showed that the squadron was Sabbatarian to a degree which would almost satisfy a Pharisee. This feeling was so strong in the Vice, whose day it was to be scullion, that he volunteered to leave until Monday all dishes needing washing, but the Purser, who succeeded him with the dish-cloth, declined to exact any such extreme test of the Vice's fidelity to the fourth commandment. A suggestion, by the Cook, that the officers should attend divine service in a body, was voted down, on the ground, that the nearest church, whose spire was plainly visible down the river, was distant more than a Sabbath day journey. (N. B. There was no wind, and to paddle back from church would be to paddle against the current.) But the Cook was determined to go to church. He shaved himself, sponged his uniform into some semblance of neatness, oiled his shoes until they lost some of their rusty look, emptied the baggy breast-pockets of his shirt, unloaded his boat, and sponged out the inside. Then he washed and smoothed a white handkerchief, the latter operation being performed by folding the kerchief, "four double," placing it between two folds of a sail, and sitting determinedly upon it for the space of half an hour. Then the Cook carefully disposed the handkerchief in his pocket, so that some inches of white corner should show against the dark blue of his shirt; he bade his slothful companions a reproachful farewell, shoved his boat from shore, and started for the sanctuary. The distance was at least five miles, the sun very hot, and the hour uncertain, but regarding the latter the Cook had some experience in guessing time rudely by the apparent altitude of the sun, so he paddled briskly along, and though he perspired freely, the fact led him to compare himself, with considerable satisfaction, with the early American settlers who endured so much discomfort rather than remain away from church, That he had no prayer-book, and was rather unfamiliar with the Mass except as a verbal accompaniment to some of his favorite music, did not distress him greatly, for in truth he was not as intent upon worship as he might have been. He had gone to church in French-American settlements in other days, and had seen how the worshippers cast off the dingy garments of the farm and shop, and appeared in bright and costly raiment, so the Cook was now going to church principally in search of the picturesque. At the end of half an hour's paddling he saw that opposite the church he was aiming for there was another, which had been hitherto hidden by the foliage upon a small island. The sacred edifices, with their dependent villages, seemed to be of equal size, and the Cook was distraught with uncertainty as to which to visit. Then along the road of one bank he saw many vehicles passing at the trot and full of people. Couldn't be?—yes, it was true—that the service at one church was over. The Cook hastily took a racing stroke, and made for the other church, which was still a mile away, but suddenly a procession of carriages appeared from that direction. The Cook dubiously paused in mid-stream, endeavored to estimate the two lines of vehicles to ascertain which was most promising; then he ran his boat ashore and scrambled up the bank. A bramble claimed his handkerchief, but he did not pause to contest the claim; he dashed across the dusty road, seated himself on the top-rail of a fence, and rigidly inspected the occupants of the vehicles until of vehicles there were no more. Then with a sigh he descended from his perch and started to paddle back, against the current, to his camp and the hungry men for whom he had to prepare dinner. Even his small measure of Sabbatarian virtue had its reward, however, for just then there came along a tug towing a barge load of lumber; under its shady side the Cook found a convenient place to tie his own boat, while from the cabin-window of the barge, the Captain's black-eyed, black-haired wife, leaned and, taking the Cook for an innocent scull-racer from Montreal, warned him impressively against "the cheats, the hogs of Yankees," who would make his life miserable if he went on to the States.

On reaching camp the Cook found the Commodore and the Vice engaged in varnishing their somewhat tarnished boats, one using brown shellac, and the other, coach varnish of the costliest description.

"Shellac," the Commodore was saying, "is certainly

inferior to your varnish in beauty of finish, but it dries in fifteen minutes, and stands water, for all that I can see, quite as well."

The Vice admitted disappointment in that the varnish which he had been at such pains to procure, turned a bluish-white color, when exposed to wet, recovering its lustre, however, on drying. This was certainly an objectionable feature, and marred the complexion of the Rochefort in a way that was highly exasperating to her owner, especially when his companions jeered him on the number of coats with which he had covered his boat.

"Look at my varnish," said the Cook finally after the others had somewhat exhausted the topic. "It is not shellac, neither is it coach varnish, yet the Cherub is arrayed in a coat which retains its lustre better than either of yours."

"What is it?"

"Even 'Pellucidite.' I know not the process whereby the lac is dissolved, which forms its basis, but it stands water better than any other that I know of, and is no more expensive than the ordinary kinds."

In fact after duly weighing the matter, the cruisers concluded that Pellucidite is the best varnish known to them for general use on canoes. It appears to be less affected by constant exposure than any other that they have tried.

"Varnishing," said the Vice, as he lay in the shade and contemplated the Rochefort glittering in the sun, "is perhaps the most ennobling way for a canoeist to spend his time after he has received his boat from the builder. Every coat you put on adds so much to her beauty. I believe I've gone over my boat in parts thirteen times."

"That's one thing that I don't like about a Chrysalid," said the Commodore. "Half your original outlay goes for fittings which it is much better fun to make yourself, and you have no recourse but to varnish and re-varnish. Now you get a Red Laker clear fore and aft—excepting two and a half feet of decking, at bow and stern, and you go to work and contrive and experiment in a manner highly stimulating to a properly organized mind, until you get her decked or covered over with a removable covering of wood or water-proof cloth, and rigged to suit you. I admit, though, that some people would rather pay more money and have less tinkering to do. Nevertheless I hold that tinkering is essentially a higher order of intellectual employment than is mere varnishing, admirable as that may be when used in moderation."

"There is enough to do in all conscience," replied the Vice, "about a Chrysalid. Look at my hatches. They consumed an enormous amount of brain force in the preparation."

As has been already stated, the Chrysalid boats have rather more than four feet of bow and stern devoted to water-tight compartments, which of course occupy a great deal of space, but are extremely useful in case of accident. These spaces the Vice had made available for light articles, such as extra clothing, etc., by cutting hatchways in his deck, and fastening them down by means of thumb-screws, the seams being rendered water-tight by strips of india rubber used as packing. Red Lakers, on the contrary, have all the room they want, but their water-tight compartments, if they have any, are only large enough for the purpose of flotation. Their owners therefore are fain to be content with water-proof bags or sheets for the protection of their haberdashery.

The charms of the natural scenery about the island finally lured the Vice away from the annotations which he was preparing for a new edition of " Jefferson's Manual," and he went with the Cook to explore a beautiful creek which emptied opposite the camp. Its charms were many, and its ways as devious as those of a woman about whom romancers write, so the couple followed it as a matter of course, until the declining sun warned them to return to their camp, but as they turned their boats' heads homeward they paddled only with leisurely strokes, so loth were they to leave the beautiful alternations of sunny hillside and shady grove, solitary giants of trees, and thickets full of birds, mats of lily pads, and bars covered with just water enough to enhance the brilliancy of their shining sands. The Cook heaved a deep sigh, and said,

" What a pity that this fair spot is where it is, among a set of peasants who are blind to its true value."

" Indeed it is," said the Vice. " There never was a

finer bit of ground for a beer garden, and such a place would call for a brewery; this, in turn, would bring out an opposition establishment, and malt and hops would look up, while coopers would find steady employment."

"Mercy!" murmured the Cook imploringly, "mercy!"

"Or," continued the Vice, "it would make a beautiful park; not large to be sure, but there is enough forest-land to clear, and enough bare land to plant with forest trees, to occupy a great many voters along about election time. Then the grades are such that the roads could be constructed only by an immense amount of work, and as there's no stone near by, the contract for road-filling would amount to a handsome thing. Properly managed, such a park would hold a party together for twenty years, unless some set of old fogies happened to impose a landscape gardener and architect upon the commissioners."

The Cook made haste to quit the creek and return to camp, and that same evening he experienced a severe bilious attack. As the Purser was already ill from a surfeit of rice and maple syrup at dinner, and the Vice was rapidly succumbing to the same viands, the Commodore charged himself with preparing a supper which should have for its principal feature an entirely new dish —to wit, fried frogs' legs. He had devised a beautiful method of taking the musical batrachians. He baited a very fine fish-hook with a bit of red flannel and affixed it to an eighty-foot trout-line. Then joining a fourteen foot rod he walked along the shady shore, and cast his line. Should the fisher for trout sneer at such outlandish fishing, and pot-fishing at that, he should know that to catch a bull-frog with hook and line requires a better eye and more skillful hand than are sufficient to successful trout-fishing. The frog never "rises" to the bait; the latter must be let gently down before his eyes and nose, and then, as he leisurely opens his jaws, be dropped into his mouth. The slightest breath of wind, or tremor of arm, causes the bait to graze the cheek of the game, and then an angry foot is lifted to brush it away, and a goggle eye rolls back reproachfully at the disturber. When the bait is taken, the frog seems to realize but slowly that anything unusual has occurred, and the sportsman is likely to accuse him of lacking the proper spirit of a game fish (or beast, or bird, whichever he may please to call it), but when the truth dawns upon the frog's mind he gives a leap, to view which would drive a kangaroo into mortification and suicide, and then goes for deep water with an alacrity which causes the reel to buzz merrily. Having tested the length of the line, however, his method changes to that of a goat, and he pulls stubbornly in a single direction while the sportsman reels him in. The Commodore illustrated this operation but once however, for after landing his first frog he was unable to find another to try his wiles upon. A few moments before, the creatures sat numerously along the water's edge, blankly blinking, and as reserved and unsympathetic as a body of officeholders at a civil service reform meeting; the spectacle of the suspension of one of their own number, however, was one which they were quick to see and take warning by.

Later in the evening the quartette received a call from a fine looking old farmer and his wife, both arriving in one of those peculiarly rotten old skiffs which, when one sees them in use, seem strong arguments in favor of a special Providence interposing to protect human life. The lady was curious to see the culinary outfit of the party, while her husband led conversation slowly but surely toward the subject of the late war in the States. When he learned that some of the party had seen military service, he manifested great satisfaction, and told of his own experiences, which the military and political exigencies of France had caused to be of varied but stirring nature. The Vice listened with a sympathy born of his recollections of the blockade-running service, but when he learned that the old fellow, when a soldier, had once fraternized with the revolutionists and fought beside them behind a barricade, he shouted, "Liberté, Egalité, Fraternité," and tumultously embraced the grizzly old warrior in true French fashion.

The next morning found the expedition still in camp upon the island, and not caring to depart. Scenery so diversified it had not been the fortune of any of the party to have seen elsewhere. Every hour of the day revealed some new beauty, and every change of light discovered new charms in those which had been seen before.

The Cook, who had become so enamored of the view that he occasionally forgot his official duties, arose at dawn one morning to enjoy the scene by sunrise. The air was chilly, so he kindled his fire and soon had a fine bed of coals behind which he stretched himself, with his face to the east. The dawn had doffed its bluish-grey night-robe and was putting on a morning-dress of soft pink, but doing it as leisurely as if this were not an age of action, and as if time were not money. Then its complexion slowly but steadily brightened under the influence of atmosphere unpolluted by factory chimney, and undisturbed by rumbling omnibus or rattling milk-wagon. It glanced kindly down into the farmer's barnyard, and received murmuring acknowledgments from the cattle and fowls; it peered between the young trees on the steep bank of the opposite shore, and each of them seemed to stand a little straighter than before, while each leaf gazed down into the watery mirror beneath and made its most elaborate toilet. The river saw it coming, and, ashamed of its own leaden complexion, hastened to throw over its face a misty veil which should prevent too close a gaze until the river's only valet should arise from his couch behind the dawn, and brighten the heavy countenance. The birds greeted cheerily the acquaintance who came every day, and whose only fault was that it never remained long enough; the tiny blossoms beneath the trees began to peer forth at it; a million daisies turned their yellow eyes toward it, and with each new attention bestowed it blushed more and more. It sent the politest of zephyrs to beg the river to remove its vail; it lavished its own charms upon the river until the stream seemed to have emerged suddenly from the fountain of youth; the most subtle and delicious perfumes diffused themselves every where, and the Cook breathed them in with a feeling that he was absorbing Nature's own sweet self. Then there floated through the air an odor more pronounced and less fragrant, and the Cook discovered that a large fold of one of his baggy trouser legs had succumbed to the attentions of the neighboring fire, and disappeared like the baseless fabric of a vision and left but a rag behind. Just then the Purser, who at home was a philosopher as well as an artist, emerged yawning from his couch and proceeded to the river and his ablutions.

"Purser," said the Cook; "you believe in the conservation of force; tell me now, I pray you, in what potent form the lost fabric of my trouser leg will reappear?"

"In a tailor's bill," replied the Purser, and the Cook, a wiser and a sadder man, sauntered off to fill the expeditionary coffee-pot.

"The squadron," remarked the Commodore, as he drained his second pint of coffee and laid aside his emptied plate, "will now prepare itself for the reception of a plain but startling statement. I call upon you all to bear witness that I did not in the least discourage the little ebullition on the part of the Cook which led him to run the rapids at the fort through the humiliating device of getting his boat carried up stream, so that he could float down. I wish now to inform the fleet that real rapids are before us. (Sensation, the squadron well knowing that naught in the nature of rapids intervened between them and the St. Lawrence.) You all know, by report at least, that the river a few miles below is crossed by a railway bridge. This railway traverses a rough section of country and shortly touches the head-waters of a wild river where they break from one of the largest of our mountain lakes. Over this road I have secured transportation for the fleet, and in two days at the latest I hope that the "Becky Sharp" will show the expedition the way down the " Horse Race " at Lake End. The stream to which I refer falls into a navigable river which in its turn joins the St. Lawrence within easy reach of transportation to New York. I have prudently kept this contemplated change of plan to myself until I could be reasonably assured of its feasibility. The letters received at the fort gave me the desired information, and I now submit my proposition to the fleet."

"We don't want to reach any where," said the Purser. "Wherever we are is paradise."

"No, we don't want to reach any where," said the Vice. "We must in some way distinguish ourselves from the tramps to whom we outwardly bear so faithful a resemblance. I'm in no hurry; my canvass for the fall elections don't begin for a month. Besides, on expeditions like this I believe, with the Alderman—"

"Wherever we are may be paradise," remarked the Cook, "but I never heard of manna being found except in the wilderness, and in my official capacity I would state that the manna of this expedition is reduced to one pair of frogs'-legs, and that these, having been gathered on the Sabbath, are, in short, spoiled."

Immediately every man began to stow his boat, and in a short time the expedition was paddling over the line of the Cook's Sabbath-day journey. At the first village touched by the squadron the Purser, who went ashore for stores, discovered that in spite of the distance from great centres of thought, the rights of woman had gained full recognition. The store was managed by a woman, who left a loom to wait upon the customer, while her husband smoked calmly in his chair and exhibited no sign of disapproval.

Nor were there lacking sufficient indications of the universal brotherhood of man. The village was as destitute of shade-trees as if it had been for years under the charge of a New Jersey road-board, and all forest trees had been as carefully removed from the broad expanse of farming land as if they had been noxious weeds. A stone pier which extended a little way into the river had cracked and settled as thoroughly as it could have done under the fostering care of a dock commission, and some people living in a house close to a large stagnant pool bewailed, as a direct visitation of Providence, the serious illness of a member of their family.

At this point the expedition admitted the advisability of obtaining from mid-stream all water for drinking and culinary purposes. They saw numerous small floats, extending fifty or more feet into the river, and at the end of each of these, (the day being Monday) bent a woman over a washtub, while at the landward end of the float a fire of driftwood burned under a kettle, and sturdy daughters of the family were engaged in tending the fire, wringing the clothes and hanging them on the bushes to dry. The beautiful simplicity of all these arrangements so impressed the Vice, that no sooner had the expedition camped on a verdant point than he remarked that he did not see why men should not wash as well as women, and extracting some articles of apparel from their hiding place, he shortly presented the appearance depicted on the following page, and now and then expressed his surprise that the fleet was not as much interested in watching his proceedings as it had been in those of the Canadian *blanchisseuses* along the water side.

It had needed but the stimulus of action to make the squadron forget its lotus-life at the island where it seemed always afternoon, and around the evening fire a healthful reaction set in favor of rapids and the contemplated change of programme.

"Use Laundry Soap and be Happy."

XII.

A CHANGE OF SCENE.

AFTER breakfast the Commodore announced that as nearly as he could estimate the town of St. Ursus was only about one hour's run from the camp, and that thence the squadron was to be shipped across country, to Lake End, a freight train being due about the middle of the morning, and a passenger train following shortly after noon. With light hearts the squadron paddled down a lovely stretch of river, past one or two " swell " houses at which the Vice looked askance, as the probable abodes of an "effete aristocracy." Two ladies, however, were encountered out rowing in a boat, and as they gave pleasant greeting to the Vice who happened to pass nearest them, his opinions underwent a marked change, and he expressed himself as not averse to associating with peeresses in their own right, as he declared these undoubtedly were.

In due time the bridge was reached; the little station at one end thereof was enlivened for a time by the presence of four canoes and their owners, the station-master showed a Montreal paper only a few hours old, the freight train thundered up and away bearing the most important part of the command, and after two or three hours of dining and loafing about, the four inferior beings followed in a passenger car. Thence an hour later they emerged and stood upon the platform at Lake End, gazing southward through a rugged mountain gateway which closed in steeply on the dark blue waters.

It was but a few minutes work to secure the services of a wagoner, who, for fifty cents, transported the four canoes one by one to the water's edge and deposited them ready for launching. By mid-afternoon the Purser and Cook had bought a few necessary supplies and the Commodore and Vice had reconnoitered the dam and scanned the rapids below, down which it was intended to run before sunset.

Very quickly the news spread through the little town that four Yankees were going down the Race, and by the time all was ready for passing the boats over a practicable part of the dam, the whole population, male and female, including summer boarders in the bewildering toilettes of the period, were ranged along the banks, with the exception of those who came to lend a hand, and a squad headed by the local hotel-keeper, who strove to dissuade the party from what he represented as a rash venture. The hotel-keeper in fact was very kind, offering to provide good rooms over night and send the boats round the Race in a wagon in the morning. But the white water was all the while roaring its invitation and drowning his arguments, and though a witness was finally brought who, having only one leg, declared that he had "run" the rapids, and that the squadron couldn't do it, the temptation was too strong to be resisted, so one after another, with safe intervals between, the cruisers paddled out into the flashing water, and then for a few minutes, with every sense on the alert, every nerve strained, no

In the Second Rapids.

one had an eye for anything save sunken rocks, treacherous swirls of the current, and the hundred indications which to the canoeist indicate the deepest water and the safest channel. It seemed only a few seconds, but the better part of a mile had been passed when the four waited for one another in the first reach of quiet water that afforded us a resting place. Each had grazed a few rocks in the first rapid, but all had passed triumphantly and without visible mishap beyond the ken of the

the hotel keeper, and the villagers, and were content. Half the Race, however, was yet to be run, and there was barely enough of daylight left for the undertaking.

> "The stream runs fast,
> The rapids are near, and the daylight past,"

sang the Purser as he paddled the Arethusela out into the stream to show the channel, the flagship following, the Cherub next, and the Rochefort bringing up the rear—an order of sequence that was presently effectually reversed. Just below the head of the next rapid the Arethusela hung upon a rock, and in an instant her commander was overboard and struggling in a fierce waist-deep current to keep his footing, and retain a hold upon his boat. To add to his discomfiture his paddle had come apart and half of it was floating merrily down the stream. As the Commodore swept past, the discomfited Purser called on him to save it; and two or three strokes brought him nearly within reach, but at the same time deflected him from the only path of safety. The next minute he, too, was in the water, which, before testing, he supposed to be knee-deep, but which proved to be nearer neck-deep, while the fugitive paddle, with a playful flourish of its blade, dived under a log, disappeared for a moment from view, and then danced cheerfully down the swift waters beyond. At this crisis the Cherub and Rochefort appeared, and flashed past as, half swimming, half wading, the two strove to reach a secure footing.

They shouted derisive inquiries for orders to the

Commodore, and presently disappeared around the bend below.

Speaking unofficially and strictly in a private capacity, the Commodore admits that he had all he could do to avoid grievous wreck on the logs beneath which his com-

Down the Race.

panion's elusive paddle had vanished. Wading and swimming were alike irreconcilable with the conditions, for the bed of the river was full of boulders over which the water boiled without breaking. He tried the plan of holding on to his boat and floating; but after being dragged and bumped for a few yards over the stones, he gave that up and resigned himself to careful wading until he reached the shallows, where he at length succeeded in re-embarking—no easy task, by the way, in swift water— and soon joined the Cherub and Rochefort.

A camping spot was selected on a bank of sawdust near which was a mighty pile of dry mill waste, and the three proceeded to light a fire and make a somewhat needful change of clothing, before getting supper and turning in for the night. After a long time the Arethu-

SAFE IN THE CAMP. 211

sela came in sight, her crew laboriously working a half-paddle—though why a spare one stowed below decks was not used was never found out—and examining the shores and channel for the lost property. This was happily discovered close to camp, and presently a "lean-to," was covered with the soaked tent, which made a reasonably comfortable shelter.

Sawdust is not so bad to sleep on when you have a boat or a rubber-blanket under you, but it retains moisture badly, and is seldom dry more than an inch below the surface. Moreover, the dry part catches fire and burns in an exceedingly persistent and stealthy manner, tunneling unsuspected in all directions and making itself very disagreeable. The members of the expedition, however, knew its nature and provided against its vagaries by wetting thoroughly in the vicinity of the fire, where the Cook speedily had coffee and a tempting pan of scrambled eggs ready for the evening meal.

The voyagers went to sleep this night with unwonted noises in their ears, namely the close-at-hand roar of rapids rising and falling as the mysterious and imperceptible changes of the evening air bore it, now heavily, now faintly, through the thick forest of spruce. It was a wilder region than that through which they had been passing on the lake and its outlet, and the woods gave out sounds at night which often aroused one and another with the pleasing and yet uncomfortable thought of bears and lynxes in his half awakened brain.

XIII.

SWIFT WATER.

HERE, at the foot of "Rapid No. 2," the authors would say a word for the benefit of the inexperienced. They are asked by cautious readers if this kind of play is not dangerous. Certainly, just as coasting, and travelling by rail, and crossing Broadway, and playing base and foot-ball, are dangerous. In short, just exactly as life itself is dangerous. They would not advise any but bold swimmers to undertake the amusement; but where proper survey is taken to avoid possible falls, a wetting is the worst that can ordinarily happen. During the entire trip no mishaps occurred save those which came in as part of the fun, and although the voyagers were wet and dry half a dozen times a day, not one caught the slightest cold, or suffered any ill effects from exposure. Hardly any woman, and not by any means all men, can be expected to appreciate the fun of these duckings and other uncertainties of canoe cruising. It may as well be admitted, however, that no out-of-door recreation that is worthy the name, is wholly without risk. The steadiest horses sometimes take fright and run away. Without its rivalries and possible perils to heart and hand, croquet itself would be but an insipid pastime. All excitement presupposes risk of some kind, but it refreshes body and brain alike when taken in reasonable doses and in a fashion that does not infringe on the rights of others. Since the Saturday afternoons of their boyhood the authors have experienced nothing so delightful as those long days on lake and river.

To certain members of the fleet the awakening in the chilly morning air, with fog rising from the water and drifting through the slender spires of balsam and spruce, was the reverse of inspiriting, and the uncertainty as to the course of the river below did not tend to create an irresistible eagerness for farther rapids and farther wettings. The sun however, soon drove away the mist, dried the heavy dew from boats and equipments, and gradually, as the river dimpled in the sunlight and rushed brimming past in a swift deep current, it resumed its attractiveness and, as soon as clothing was dry enough to put on, every man was eager to begin the day's adventures, and get it comfortably wet again.

Single file should be the order of procedure in a rapid river where there is any question as to the width of unobstructed channel. On sighting a rapid whose foot cannot be clearly seen from its head, some one should reconnoitre, and after noting the bearings of the current, should lead the way, the rest of the fleet following at safe intervals and taking prompt warning from his example in case he comes to grief. As a general rule the water is deepest near the *concave* shore. The reason is obvious. Each general shore-line of a crooked stream is a series of points and bays modified by a hundred varying conditions. Every point tends to deflect the current toward the opposite shore, and where the strongest current is, there is ordinarily the deepest water. Where the stream breaks into rapids the same rule holds good, but is liable to endless modifications from boulders and rocks of all shapes and sizes. Nevertheless it may be assumed that it has been trying for untold ages to shape its channel according to nature's rule, and it will be found in most cases to have attained a reasonable success. At the head of a rapid the white broken water is almost invariably V shaped, the apex pointing down stream. Between the arms of the V the water is comparatively smooth, and dark. Along the arms and below the apex is white water, thrown up more or less into waves. It is generally the safest course, barring casual rocks which may put in an appearance anywhere, to head directly for the apex of the V, keeping in unbroken water as long as possible. Then trust to luck and a quick eye and hand to avoid the rocks which come too near the surface. Nothing but experience can teach one to recognize these, and even recognition does not always imply the ability to avoid disaster.

If a keel-boat hangs resolutely on an obstacle, there is nothing for its occupant to do but to jump overboard, and the quicker the better, if he wishes to keep his stores dry. In many cases such a boat may swing free or be lifted clear by a powerful thrust of the paddle. The canoeist's instinct is all that he has to tell him whether to jump or thrust. With a keelless canoe the case is different as it is comparatively rare that such an one will hang persistently to an obstacle. It is often best however, to take to the water in order to save the canoe from hard knocks and scrapes. In view of this necessity for jumping overboard, some protection is necessary for the feet, and there is nothing so good as the common canvas bathing-shoes with thick soles of hemp or jute. An old pair of slippers is, however, far better than nothing.

Upon the whole, the best policy is to sit as usual amidships and give to rocks the widest berth possible. There is a pernicious doctrine in some quarters, derived it must be confessed from English canoeists, that in running rapids it is well to sit astride the canoe near the stern, and lift her clear if she strikes by simply standing up on the bottom of the stream, if it can be reached with the feet. The Purser tried this once, purely out of patriotism, but did not make a very good demonstration of its advantages, for he upset as soon as he ran out of shoal water, or rather he took a ducking in order to save his stores which would inevitably have been wet had he tried for an instant longer to maintain his precarious seat. The rivers of Europe may admit of this very unpicturesque mode of running a rapid, but those of America do not take to it kindly.

The keels of the Chrysalids, are a decided disadvantage in this phase of canoeing. They give the canoe additional draught, and hang with provoking tenacity upon any rock or other obstacle which they encounter. The Red-Lakers on the contrary slide with an inch or more to spare over an obstacle which would bring a Chrysalid to instant grief. They turn far more easily, and hence can much more readily be made by a quick swerve to one side or the other, to avoid a threatened danger. The blindest worshipper of the Chrysalid model can claim nothing for a keel in swift water, save that it receives the hard knocks which would otherwise have scarified the more fragile bottom planks. This argument in their favor is not good for much, as the keel cannot protect more than two or three inches on each side, unless the obstacle happens to be broad and flat. Under these conditions, it was to be expected that the Rochefort would select with excellent judgment a place whereon to demonstrate the advantages of her keel. It may have been at the foot of Rapid No. 9, at any rate it was at the head of a comparatively quiet reach of water where three of the fleet had drawn out of the current with a view to luncheon. The Vice was the last to arrive, and was sweeping boldly down where the current was swift and deep, having passed the white water, when suddenly he was observed to bring up all standing, his boat swinging round instantly across the current, having fixed a malicious grip upon a hidden rock, over which the water boiled, but did not break. The Vice was unceremoniously plumped out on the down-stream side into water that was neck deep and running like a mill-race, but as he wore a life-belt he feels justified in maintaining that he did not go entirely under. He succeeded in getting a hold upon the rock by the aid of his boat hook, and seated himself thereon, holding his boat by the painter as she floated, full of water and only sustained by her air-tight compartments, a yard or two below him. The picture that he presented at this moment was comical in the extreme, and he was heartlessly kept sitting there,—he could not very well get off alone with his boat to manage,—while the Commodore made a sketch. The regular artist was too much concerned at his friend's critical situation to pay any attention to the calls made upon him for a careful study. The current was so swift and deep that efforts to reach the Vice by swimming were unsuccessful, so it became necessary to wade out a few rods below him and catch his boat, when he let her float down. He easily swam ashore when relieved of this charge, and once more the Rochefort had to be emptied of everything, and all lay by for two or three hours, while her owner and his belongings were spread out on the rocks to dry, he discoursing, the while, until all fell asleep, of the innate viciousness of a boat which could thus deliberately bring her commander to confusion and shame.

It was in "Number 12" that all came nearest to utter discomfiture, that is to actual overturns, and consequent wettings of things not intended to be wet. Never had

The Vice sits for his Portrait.

the Vice, whose turn it was to survey the route, seen a more innocent-looking rapid. It swept down in a slight curve, dancing in the sun and seemingly offering a clear channel. It was the flagship's turn to bring up the rear, and in watching the descent of the others the Commodore perceived that at a certain point each crew of one became as it were demoralized, and struggled mightily with the current until each turned at a right angle and went on its way into the pool below. The reason was not apparent until he reached the same point, when he suddenly became aware that the stream was bearing him with great velocity directly upon a huge rock. To go to starboard was certain wreck. The only safety lay in turning sharply to port, as his predecessors had done. To all appearance this was utterly impossible, and, while straining every nerve to make good his escape, the flag-officer fully expected to be rolled over into twelve feet of water in the most undignified manner, and in full view of the fleet. Just at the last moment, when an overturn seemed inevitable, an unexpected set-back from the rock caught the canoe and whirled her instantly over a delightful little dip, hardly high enough to be termed a fall, into the deep water below, where the rest of the fleet lay enjoying the perplexity and relief through which each in his turn had passed. It is quite impossible under such circumstances to shout advice, for the roar of the water completely overpowers the voice. What would have happened if any or all had struck the rock? Why, each and all would have been spilled comfortably into deep water, to be sure, whence it would have been easy to swim ashore and put things to rights.

After a day of exciting work of this kind it was not unpleasant in the afternoon to paddle out upon the smooth waters of a little lake in the midst of the forest. Along its gentle swelling shores were scattered farm houses, beyond which the rough clearings crept up the hillsides. Two or three huge water-oaks bent over the shore in a shady cove, and here the squadron took shelter until the sun's rays should be less vertical. Presently from a neighboring farm house there came down to the water's edge a damsel who proceeded artlessly to rivet upon herself the attention of the fleet by lighting a fire under a boiler, and doing up the family washing at the lake-side. The artist filled a page or two of his sketch-book with studies from the life, but refuses for some reason to furnish them for publication. She was near enough, however, to afford a fine opportunity, as the Artist said, to study the peculiar French type of form and feature, as modified by several generations of life in a foreign climate.

Presently the Commodore, under pretence of inquiring after eggs and milk, approached *la blanchisseuse*. The Cook lounged respectfully behind his commanding officer, while the latter addressed the woman in alleged French to receive only a dismal shake of the head in reply. He repeated his question, changing the phraseology, but with a different result, while the Cook, to relieve the Commodore's evident embarrassment, softly whistled the Thuringian "Volks-lied." A pleased glance from the woman elicited a word or two from the Cook; after a short but spirited conversation in which the Commodore took no part, the Cook informed his companion that the desired supplies could be had at the house, and the two men departed.

"Confound this French lingo!" exclaimed the Commodore, "there are as many dialects in this region as there are towns, and I don't easily pick them up; how do *you* manage to do it?"

"My dear fellow," said the Cook impressively, "there is one rule to be unvaryingly observed in conversing with these people : never speak French to a woman who understands only the German language."

The Commodore dropped the milk-pail—fortunately it was empty—and endeavored to swear the Cook to secrecy, with what success this narrative doth show. But he derived some consolation from frequent allusions to the Purser's professional studies of the "French type of form and feature, as modified by a change of abode."

When the sun was low enough to cast the shadow of the hills upon the lake, the fleet started and made its way toward a distant point which, it was surmised, was not far from the outlet and would afford good camping ground for the night. A more delightful three mile paddle can hardly be imagined. The peculiarly sacred stillness of a forest-land at sunset was over all the scene; a silence that seemed absolute, and was yet vocal with noises that did not break the spell. The plash of leaping fish, the far off scream of an eagle, the occasional laughter of a loon, the measured dip of paddles, none of these were discordant with nature, and even the human tones that now and then floated from the distant houses were so faint as to be inoffensive. The voyagers hardly exchanged a word as side by side they slid through the reflected hues of sunset, watching in silence the mighty mountain that rose in dark purple against the west, and gathered around its summit a night-cap of cloud that changed from red to grey just as the point was reached and the tent pitched beneath a huge gnarled pine, that towered above its fellows, and offered, as the Vice suggested, an admirable mark for any nocturnal thunderstorm that might be wandering in this direction. Only one thing aroused any apprehensions as to the comfort of this camp, and that was the ceaseless roar (the word is used advisedly in preference to "hum") of insects. They proved innocuous, however, and sleep soon came down upon the tired canoeists.

XIV.

MORE RAPIDS.

CONTRARY to custom the camp had been pitched where the morning sun would strike in upon it. This is undesirable unless an early start is the order of the day, for breakfast in the level rays of a summer sun is not so comfortable as in the shade of a natural screen. At a tolerably seasonable hour, therefore, the squadron paddled around the point and across the reach which still separated them by two miles or so from the outlet. For variety the wind was dead ahead, but the distance was soon passed and the flash of rapids at the very lip of the lake announced that the stream maintained the character which it had displayed in the earlier portion of its career. In a moment the four pretty canoes were in line at ample distance apart and were dancing down the swift current into a dark sweep of spruce-covered banks, with four as light hearted vagabonds on board as ever left care behind them.

In retrospect it is hardly possible to recall any part of this romantic river where a halt was not a luxury merely because of the picturesque surroundings. Seldom could the eye reach more than half a mile up or down stream, for the precipitous or forest-covered banks were continually pushing out on the one side and receding on the other, while between them the river curved and wound in a perpetual succession of rapids, pools, and quiet stretches. The current even in its most quiet moods was singularly swift and powerful, bearing the fleet onward with hardly an effort, at the rate of six or seven miles an hour. When clearings occurred they were on the points, as is always the case in thinly settled countries. Naturally such points are formed in the re-entrant angle of the stream, and become places of deposit for drift and alluvium in flood time. The opposite bank is usually bold and with soil enough in most cases to sustain only the wild forest growth. The quiet reaches, however, are frequently broken where the river forces its way through narrow passages, or over rocky ledges. There are no dangerous falls until within a mile of the mouth, and there is only one dam between the lake and the falls. This dam the voyagers reached a few hours after leaving the lake; hours full of the pleasant, healthful excitement of rapids and wild shifting scenery.

Striking the back-water of the mill-pond a mile above the dam, the fleet paddled down and soon came in sight of the logs and crib-work which indicate the presence of a saw-mill.

Drawing up alongside the boom, all hands walked across the dam and considered the chances of running the race-way. Noon had passed however, and while the question was still unsettled, children came down from the mill-settlement with fresh raspberries, and butter made in the French style, without salt, and thus reminded of luncheon, it was decided, in view of an approaching thunder shower, to adjourn to the shelter of the mill. Here an incident occurred which proved as it had never been proved before the admirable discipline maintained in the *personnel* of the command.

In the early days of the cruise it became painfully evident to the real canoeists who were connected with the expedition, that in one particular at least an unseemly tendency toward effeminate luxury was developing itself. The Vice and the Purser, on the first day out, produced with an air of insufferable superiority, china plates, and bowls which they were pleased to denominate coffee cups. The relative size of these as compared with the legitimate tin-cups used by the Commodore and the Cook is herewith shown. Of course the flag-officer at once detected the ruse, and foiled the conspirators by issuing at the first camp, Special Order No. 1 to this effect:

> The coffee ration will always be measured in the Cook's cup, that being the standard pint recognized at these headquarters.
> By order of the Commodore.

Possible infringement on the rights of individuals having thus been provided against, it was only necessary to counteract so far as possible the demoralizing effect of the daily sight of china upon the morale of the expedition. This end was diligently sought by the commanding officer by every means in his power, but to no purpose. He personally supervised the daily measuring of coffee with the Cook's cup, but by some means the china bowls were always filled, and their owners never failed to remark upon the superior excellence of coffee taken from such receptacles over that imbibed from barbaric tin. It was

Comparative Coffee Cups.

evident that sooner or later a resort must be had to arbitrary measures, but no fitting opportunity presented itself until the squadron took refuge in the mill as narrated above.

The thunder storm proved to be of extraordinary violence, throwing down trees, overturning buildings and playing the mischief generally.

Midway of the meal the wind so increased as to drive the rain in upon the festive board. The Commodore saw that the time had come for action, and acted with the promptitude which should always characterize an able commander. "Prepare for a change of base," he shouted above the roar of rain and wind. "*Purser*, coffee-pot and sugar; *Vice*, devilled turkey and salt; *Cook*, bread and butter." Each man seized the articles indicated and fled to a place of shelter. With a gleam of triumph in his eye the Commodore collected the remaining dishes, and taking his life in his hand, for the good of the service, sprang upon a pile of logs that was awaiting the saw, and attempted to cross it at a run. At the third step a log tilted. The Commodore went down, while the spasmodic upward motion of the arms, under such circumstances, sent the dishes aloft. They speedily came down, but it was in pieces that did the Cook's heart good to see. The Commodore, it is true, might have broken his leg, but he did not, and while he somewhat ruefully rubbed his starboard shin, he watched with scarce concealed satisfaction the gathering of the fragments. Not a bowl or a plate remained. The morale of the expedition was saved!

After the storm passed, it became necessary to circumvent or run the dam. It was a logging dam, some eighteen feet in perpendicular height, and offered extraordinary inducements for running, but with a little too much risk, so the boats were laboriously passed one by one over the wing of the dam, and found themselves at the head of a superb rapid which swept beneath and around a rocky cape, and quickly carried the fleet beyond the ken of the little forest settlement lying around the mill.

If possible the scenery below the mill was more picturesque than any previously seen. At one point the woods were on fire, and for a few hundred yards the smoke was so thick that progress had to be made with extreme caution, as the current was swift and the channel full of rocks. At another the stream wound slowly between wood-crowned cliffs, whose geological nature severely taxed the scientific attainments of the expedition, and tempted a long sojourn, while the Artist vainly essayed a realistic sketch of the strangely convoluted strata, which made the face of the cliff so wonderfully expressive of the elemental strife and torture that must have shaped it in some by-gone age. So with alternating reaches of swift and still water, the lovely stream coursed downward, bearing the fleet only too rapidly toward its junction with the larger river. One more night was passed among the spruces of its rugged shores, and shortly after the next morning's start it became evident that the forest stream was preparing to fulfill its destiny in driving the saws of a great mill. Houses straggled along the bank, and presently the fleet was feeling its way among logs and booms to a landing place. A few hours sufficed to procure transportation around the beautiful falls, and by sundown the squadron was making camp as usual on the banks of a broad placid river, which to all appearances was the same which it left a few days before. Here was Acadia again, and something of a mental effort was necessary to realize that it was another Acadia from that wherein the first æon of the cruise had passed. The vesper bell sounded as before, the lumber laden barges drifted as lazily as ever, and the villages named after unheard of saints dotted the banks in close succession, and the roar of rapids was no longer to be heard.

XV.

THE BEGINNING OF THE END.

IT had been something of a relief to stow masts and sails compactly away for a few days, and now again it was an agreeable change to be once more under canvas and see the slender masts bend and spring before the breeze.

In the course of a day's sail the river narrowed perceptibly, as rivers are wont to do as they near their outlets, and the various members of the expedition, having noted the fact, proceeded, each in his own way, to discover the cause thereof. A melancholy howl (learned from Garibaldians in Italy) by the Vice, who was always in the rear, was rightly construed by the occupants of the Red Lakers (in the advance) as a sign that the Vice wanted to light his pipe, so the Cook, who by virtue of his official position was custodian of the expeditionary matches, lay to until the Vice came alongside.

"The river," remarked the Vice, between puffs, "is narrowing—every mile. Suppose it—should keep on—doing it for—fifty miles more; it—would close entirely before—it reached the—ow!—(here the flame of the match reached the Vice's fingers)—reached St.—the devil, oh!" for the Vice had dropped the still blazing fragment upon his bare foot.

"No such saint in any calendar but that of politics," said the Cook reprovingly.

"The St. Lawrence, I meant, of course," said the Vice: "the devil isn't recognized by *any* party at all."

"I suppose not," answered the Cook, who had dropped into a dreamy reverie. "The true workers in this world are never recognized by those who are most entirely dependent upon them."

"You're begging the question," exclaimed the Vice, examining his scorched instep. "An apology in the shape of your flask of olive oil will be satisfactory. How *do* you explain the river's shrinking, any how?"

"Why, it's growing deeper, and as there's only a given amount of water, it can't occupy more space in one direction without narrowing in another. It's a precedent you might safely follow in politics."

The Vice reflected for a moment; then a sweet smile irradiated his features, his left eye closed, his right forefinger was slowly laid athwart his nose, and he replied,

"I knew that long ago, my boy; it's the mainstay of the business—the system, I mean. Let the party broaden, and 'Othello's occupation's gone.'"

But the Cook, having relieved his mind of chaff which nevertheless carried (unknown to him) a grain of wheat, determined to inflict upon some one else the questioning to which he had been subjected, so he speedily overhauled the other Chrysalid containing the Purser, and demanded the reason of the river's narrowing. The Purser abruptly ceased patching a sonnet which he had scribbled upon the blade of a spare paddle, and answered,

"The water-drops, so long united, have a premonition of the doom of separation soon to befall them, and they cling more closely to each other, for a last fond interchange of sentiment."

"Water is not compressible by its own volition," promptly replied the Cook, who loved cyclopedias, and never knew sentiment when he encountered it. But the Purser, who hated questions so intensely that, had he lived in the time of that vigorous old interrogation point yclept Socrates, would have tramped a thousand miles for hemlock rather than have left the sage unpoisoned, ran ashore to avenge himself upon the Commodore, who had beached his boat to await the coming up of his lagging fleet. To the commanding officer the Purser put the disturbing question as to the cause of the narrowing of the river, and with the following result:

"Rivers shrink toward their natural channel for the same reason that capitalists take to government bonds—because their banks are slippery, and suffer by the many rushes upon them."

The villages grew nearer together as rapidly as the shores did, and ahead and aloft there were always in sight several church spires of the unvarying pattern peculiar to churches along the river. Every spire was metal-covered and bright, the latter perhaps because there were no opposition houses of worship to cause that dismalness of aspect affected by all churches in neighborhoods where religion tends more to squabbling than to sanctity. At short intervals appeared the residences of the priests, each indicated by a tall cross at the gateway. The Commodore, with his peculiar regard for the church so near a sister to his own, signified a half-intention to go ashore to confession, but on being reminded that but a week remained for the cruise, and that no such short time would suffice an editor in which to unburden his soul of its manifold sins and transgressions, he forbore to make others suffer for his own faults. It was noticed thereafter, however, that he doffed his helmet respectfully whenever he sailed past a church, and that when his own day for foraging came, he preferred always to purchase milk from a priest's housekeeper.

About this time the Purser began to drop behind in a manner inexplicable even by the known slowness of his boat; even the slow-sailing Vice distanced him, so the Cook, not without a special appreciation of the Purser's tobacco, went ashore to wait for his comrade to come up. The bank of the river was high, and the Cook, who had been hugging the shore for shade, had made company for himself by roaring sundry staves, supposing that no one but his comrades were within listening distance. Great was his surprise, therefore, when on clambering up the bank he beheld a closely built village in front of him.

Had the locality been any but Acadia, even the river banks could not have hidden the town, but here the dwellings are as modest of mien as the natives. Few boast of a second story, nor is the floor of the first very much raised above the level of the ground. In exterior dimensions, most of the houses reminded the Cook of his chicken-house at home, or of those suburban villas which cluster so thickly upon the hills adjoining Central Park. But with size the last-named parallel ceased, for the exteriors were painted, the floors, seen through the open doors and windows, were clean, and no pig disported himself about the door-step. Children clustered about them as thickly as they always do about very small houses, but the matrons lacked that fagged, heaven-hungry mien peculiar to their sisters in climes where the Scripture is fulfilled by the greatest being the servant of all—all of her own servants. Here one might speak of love in a cottage and not be laughed out of society—hopeless, indeed, would be his fate were he to desire any other sort of asylum for his affections.

The Cook longed for social intercourse in this real Acadia, but he doubted the ability of his French to see him through; fortunately he espied a shop, and therein he purchased sundry sticks of candy; with one of these gravitating between his fingers and lips, he strolled about, and within five minutes he had enchained in sweet bonds several lapsful of dark-eyed children whose pure intuitions taught them that in the great human search for sweetness and light it was never well to decline a proffered half of the desirable whole.

When the Purser drew near, it was with a sketch-book loaded with drawings of odd boats which had been passed at their moorings; and the names of these, with those of their owners, which were painted in antique letters astern, would have been of inestimable value to any writer of a French romance. And he brought something dearer yet to the eyes and heart of the Cook, and yet not wholly unpicturesque, it being a pair of cockerels, handsomely spangled, which he had purchased of a thrifty dame with whom he had exchanged some courteous words as he lounged past her riparian laundry in his boat. The Cook hastily took to his boat, distanced the Commodore and Vice, and an hour later announced broiled chickens for dinner, the gridiron having been a few feet of stout wire, which after use could be crumpled together into a thin handful of old iron, yet extended, at need, to a two-chicken capacity.

After the expedition had dined, each member discovered, upon arising, that the human side is not destitute of muscles, and that a steady strain of half a day at rudder and paddle, can search these out in a manner as uncomfortable as it is thorough. The Purser, who usually made himself conspicuous, when ashore, by a broad red woolen sash, apparently a muffler such as small boys wear upon their necks in winter, was by far the most agile of the party, and his companions, as they rubbed away the stitches in their sides, inwardly vowed that the picturesque was not always ridiculously useless, particularly when assumed on proper occasions, instead of being treated as of constant utility.

As the wind was gaining in industry, the Commodore permitted an overlong delay, to be improved physically, and while this was being enjoyed there hove in view a craft peculiar to French-American waters, but which would not be tolerated anywhere else. It was an immense barge, considerably more awkward than a canal boat, and moved by two great square sails, each with a mast to itself. The breeze which bellied the canvas of this monster would have driven a canoe along at the rate of twelve miles an hour, but the barge proceeded so leisurely that a maiden sauntering along the road on the bank chatted with the pilot for a mile or two without quickening her pace. Having both his vessel and his sweetheart upon his mind, it is not strange that the pilot did not perceive the four foreign craft beached a-starboard; the maiden, however, with a woman's eye for color, caught sight of the club signal which the Cook always flew at his masthead, instead of upon the main-peak, with which it would have been furled when sail was taken in. Her figure, which had afforded so gracious a relief against the blue sky behind her, disappeared with the unscientific effect of seeming to leave a cloud behind, and as the unintentional listeners devoutly thanked heaven for such knowledge of the French tongue as had enabled them to overhear the artless affectionate dialogue which had been going on, they saw, gazing at the pilot, how dark the Acadian complexion can be when displayed in the face of a lover newly made lonesome. Gladly would the swain himself have retired from sight, but the helm of his boat was obedient only under greatest effort, so he strained sullenly at the tiller, a figure at first amusing but soon pathetic. The sentiment which keeps the world from growing old was not a stranger to the canoeists, so the Purser murmured a bit from Jasmin and caught a hint which for years he had tried to take from Jules Breton ; the Cook wished there might be a joint of chicken left to offer the poor fellow ; the Commodore hailed him heartily, and offered to carry him out a taste of brandy in token of a professional and sentimental sympathy, and the Vice sent him a good cigar ; and it came to pass that five minutes later the ere-while lovelorn helmsman was trolling a song of war and slaughter as merrily as if love and Evangeline had never existed.

"Ah," sighed the Commodore, "the days are gone when rum and true religion were the principal supports of fallen humanity. Smoke seems to answer that fellow's purpose as well as religion."

"If my memory serves me rightly," said the Vice, as if in profound reflection, "a great deal of the religion I have heard preached, was well informed with a something from which smoke is a natural deduction."

"That," said the Purser, "is because in the universal

fitness of things a man recalls most readily that which he most urgently needs. No one can wonder that a politician—"

"Language unparliamentary," interrupted the Vice, with a wry face.

"A statesman, then," resumed the Purser, "should recall most vividly the only element by which he can effectually be purified."

"Sulphur is not to be used under the rays of the sun," interposed the Commodore; "let's take to a more cooling element."

A few moments were devoted to extra-careful stowing, for there was a likelihood that *terra firma* would again be reached only on the shores of the great St. Lawrence. The Vice, with the statesmanlike instinct of saving himself by assisting his companions heavenward, endeavored by fair means and foul to persuade the others to accommodate his gun, shot-bag and the volume of Tupper, but regarding the latter his failure was complete. At length he slyly tossed it into the branches of an umbrageous ash, a picturesque old landmark of centuries. But the Commodore saw him, and went handsomely to the rescue of the old tree by knocking the book out with a boat-hook.

"There are trees enough being destroyed daily by coon-hunters, road-boards, and other villains," said he, "and I won't stand quietly by and see so splendid a specimen crushed beneath so relentless a weight."

"But somebody may find the book," pleaded the Vice, who was already afloat.

"Thank heaven, the natives can't read English," replied the Commodore, "so they won't be injured."

"But I supposed I might find it there when I came this way on next summer's cruise," said the Vice.

"So you will," said the Commodore; "neither wind nor wave can move any thing so heavy: when that book changes its base, there'll be nothing left to cruise with, and nobody left to cruise."

The Commodore, for reasons which he would not explain, had ordered that the St. Lawrence should be reached that day, even though there was not a breath of wind, and the whole trip had to be made under paddle, and the Cook knew full well that when a Commodore (or any-one else) issues an order that sounds well and prints nicely, its success or failure depends largely upon the digestion of those who are expected to execute it. So the Cook prepared a meal as digestible as it was bountiful, and within an hour the expedition had consumed enough of omelettes, stewed potato, rice croquettes, cream-toast and coffee to have terrified their respective wives into applying for divorces on the ground of inordinate appetite.* It is barely possible that the meal was prolonged with the hope that a breeze might spring up in the meantime,

---

* NOTE BY THE COMMODORE.—The Cook's notoriously fertile imagination has misled him slightly in regard to this *menu*. But let it stand. The Commodore, however, wishes to state that salt-pork and hard-tack formed the staple of the repast so far as he was personally concerned.

and do away with the necessity not only of paddling, but of taking down and stowing away all standing rigging, which in still water is likely to unfavorably affect the time of the boat. But no breeze came, not even in reply to some vigorous whistling on the part of the Commodore. So the expedition took to its several paddles, and got into mid-stream to get all possible assistance from the current, and then, just where the river was widest, and the squadron furthest from shore, a brisk breeze came down as unexpectedly as if it were a savings bank, and each man had to paddle ashore again to re-step his masts so that he could set his sail. Then the squadron ran rapidly down the river, wondering only if such a breeze on so small a water could work a man up to so keen an ecstacy, how they would be able to contain themselves when cruising upon the almost shoreless St. Lawrence.

As usual,* the Cook, in the Cherub, soon took the lead, and rapidly increased the distance between himself and his companions. There was nothing to fear, for the Vice, who had previously been through the river with the Alderman, had assured the party that there was not another rapid between it and the St. Lawrence. And even if there should be one which the Vice had forgotten, the Cook would be glad of the geographical ignorance which would enable him to shoot it without the attendance of three other boats, with their advisory counsels. So he hauled his main-sail close and flew along through

* Note by the rest of the Squadron—" As usual—Ha ha !"

the water, his steering-paddle keeping upon his wrist a strain more delicious than man ever felt at the larger end of a trout-rod. He shouted, he whistled, and finally, there being no critic within hearing distance, he sang. And as his rather uncertain voice rose and fell, the wind seemed to supply a deep bass, a foundation into which his wavering notes fitted perfectly. He fervently thanked the wind, and the tall trees through which it roared, for their sympathetic effort; he redoubled his own vocal exertions, and the wind and trees, apparently touched by his appreciation, seemed to assist more heartily than before. Suddenly the Cook noticed that the east bank, from which direction the wind came, was without trees at that point, and while he dropped into silence to wonder how the sound could be created where the means were lacking, the bass turned gradually to sub-bass. Suddenly he saw an irregularly intermitting spout of water near the middle of the river, then he noticed a troubled wrinkle across the river's entire front. He hastily let his boat come up into the wind and run into what seemed a cove on the east bank, and as she ran ashore there arose a loud shout of applause from a dozen men congregated there.

"No one ever came so near before," said one, in French.

"Saved by a minute!" ejaculated another.

"Could he have meditated suicide?" murmured a third. "No; he looks not like one who has been disappointed in love."

The Cook courteously but firmly demanded an explanation, and one of the bystanders, a venerable man in the dusty coat of a miller, led him to a slight elevation to obtain it. Then the Cook saw that a natural and abrupt fall of about fifteen feet extended entirely across the river! In an instant he vowed a handsome subscription to the campaign fund of whatever candidate might run against the Vice in the autumn campaign.

The other boats approached in the order of their rapidity, the Chrysalids coming last, and the Vice's admission that his boat, with its keel, could never have escaped had it been in the Cherub's dangerous proximity to the falls, so reacted upon the Cook's temper that he alienated a portion of the intended subscription to the opposition campaign fund, and expended it upon a dinner for four, for which he gave the proprietress of an adjoining hotel—"*Le Hotel de la Ville*"—*carte blanche*. And the landlady did her best. For an hour she and several assistants hung over two stoves, while other assistants scoured the neighborhood for delicacies. The dinner was appetizing, as was all whereof the squadron partook in Acadia after they had learned to avoid the railroad hotels. Finally after all else was disposed of, an immense dish of raspberries was placed upon the table, and beside it a small bowl full of what seemed to be buttermilk.

"There!" exclaimed the Vice, eying the bowl with manifest disgust, " that's an illustration of the effect of monarchical institutions upon physical habits. The dinner has been perfect, thus far, but now, just when the climax should be attained, they offer us buttermilk!"

"Perhaps it's cream," suggested the Commodore.

"Cream?" said the Vice scornfully. "Oh no. I know cream. Cream is a thin blue fluid. This is not like it in the least."

Here the Vice scooped a teaspoonful of the pasty fluid, and brought it gently towards his fastidious nose. Suddenly he tasted it, straightened rigidly, and exclaimed,

"Judas Iscariot! It *is* cream!"

The Vice said no more until he had sampled the bowl to the extent of a saucerful. Then he raised his face and displayed unwonted lines of thoughtfulness and conviction, as he exclaimed,

"Gentlemen, if an English cow gave that cream, I have no hesitation in saying that our independence wasn't worth fighting for!"

"Huzza!" shouted the Commodore and the Purser, as they fell into each other's embrace and wept conservative tears upon each other's blue shirt-collars, while the sternly patriotic Cook pushed the seductive bowl afar and whistled the "Star-Spangled Banner," as a counter-irritant. But when he asked for his bill, and found that it was but thirty-five cents for each individual, he retired to the hotel parlor where there was an asthmatic cottage-organ and penitently played "Rule, Britannia," keeping, however, a cautious foot upon the soft pedal lest his temporary lapse from national love should be discovered.

On returning to the boats it was discovered that the small boy who had been engaged as watchman had accumulated half a hundred deputies. As none of these expected any money, the fickle Vice fluctuated back to his first love among the nations, and was rebuked by the Commodore for judging all things by a financial standard.

The breeze had apparently been to dinner too, for it was amazingly reinvigorated and marked about forty flaws to the hour. An order to carry only "dandy" sails was protested against by the entire command, and the Commodore, hoping that the coffin trade was not depressed in the shipping port at the river's mouth, reluctantly gave way to the wishes of his subordinates. The result was that extraordinary time was made, and twenty-five miles were passed almost before the voyagers realized that the afternoon was waning.

As they approached the close of their voyage, the the considerable town where their voyage was to end, it occurred to the squadron that its personal and individual appearance was the reverse of prepossessing. A halt was accordingly made, and for an hour assiduous attention was paid to baths, soap, shaving utensils, and the carefully preserved remnants of what had once been laundried articles of wear. The one pocket mirror had long since disappeared, so that certain delicate operations of the toilette were performed with some uncertainty. The Commodore had reached the final touches, and was tenderly arranging the thin locks which still cluster about his posterior cranial processes. To this task he devoted for a time all the powers of his gigantic intellect, but in the absence of the accustomed mirror, the result was unsatisfactory. Dropping his hand at last, the Commodore sighed, and looked around for assistance. The Vice, resplendent in a white shirt and neck-tie, was unoccupied. To him the Commodore, tendering the fragmentary comb:

"I say, Vice, part my hair, will you, please."

The Vice marveled, but mechanically took the comb, while the Commodorial dome was bowed conveniently before him. Long he paused, so long that the Commodore, losing patience, called out, "Why don't you go ahead?"

"My dear boy," said the Vice, "So I would, but there's nothing in the world to part."

The venerable mariner slowly straightened himself, looked blankly for a moment into the face of his lieutenant, and passed his hand reflectively over the smooth top of his head.

"I beg your pardon, boys," he said at last. "I had forgotten. This cruise has made me so much younger that I thought I wasn't bald yet. It's high time for me to be back at the office—'There'll be no parting there.'"

Of the remainder of the run, some five or six miles, no member of the squadron is mentally fitted to give a correct account. Every one wanted to be first in port, and the Vice, in anticipation of being the fortunate man, had secretly extemporized a new star spangled banner to carry at the peak of his mainsail. But both Red Lakers shot ahead of the Chrysalids, and the Vice at last ignominiously took in his national ensign because it wasted a certain amount of wind.* Finding there was but one boat against him, the Cook assumed that he had himself already won the race, so he began to compose a sarcastic address to be delivered to his associates as one by one they rejoined him at whatever landing-place he might select. While he composed he heard a whiz, he saw a shadow, and the wind died (apparently) so suddenly that he barely had time to adjust the trim of his boat to avoid capsizing. Looking about him he saw the great sails of the flagship passing him to windward, and he heard the voice of the Commodore, in tones which no combination of type can express, shouting,

"Come to the best hotel and see me when you get in!"

So the Cook looked about for some excuse to make for what would be his probable tardiness, and he soon found it. As he flew past a large assemblage of rafts, he found their occupants, all Canadians, in an extreme fever of curiosity to know how the boats were steered; the wind being from their own bank, they could not see the steering-oar on the opposite side. They also looked upon the Red Lake boats, built in their own country, as utter

* The astute congressman who occasionally enables the eagle to scream may find a valuable precedent in this act of the Vice.

strangers, which fact enabled the Cook to moralize, by comparison, upon the ignorance of people about their own neighbors, and upon the peculiar fancies which in such cases are made to do duty as facts. The Cook explained to the full extent of his knowledge and his French, and then, sighting the Chrysalids within a mile he sheared away, and within five minutes a swell from a steamer sent a wave of St. Lawrence water under his bows, and he saw the "Great Lone River of the North," from the midst of as entangling an alliance of steamers, barges, tugs, schooners, ferry-boats, yachts, fishing boats and pirogues as any canoe was ever imperilled of, while the Commodore lay under the lee of a decayed pier, and placidly smoked at his subordinate's confusion.

The St. Lawrence was hailed with delight by the tardy Chrysalids when they reached it, and then the party strolled to the post office, debating whether to run up to Montreal, which course the wind favored, or down to Quebec, with the current and an occasional tide to help. All admitted that the cruise had but fairly begun; placid lakes and beautiful rivers were all very well, but,

> "Give to them the roaring seas
> And the white waves heaving high,"

or as much thereof as was within the bestowal of a river many miles across. Just then they reached the post-office, their change of course deprived them of mail matter for several days. How it came about, nobody knew; but within an hour the Commodore, his boat stowed for return as freight, was on a train for New York, and his comrades were mourning that they could not accompany him. That evening all the canoes were stowed, and placed on board a south-bound canal-boat, while the Vice, the Purser and the Cook sat in Christian garb upon the deck of the Montreal steamer, smoked cigars instead of pipes, and discussed dados, symphony concerts, the woman question, the railroad riots, and the impending finance muddle as conventionally as if they had never lived out of doors.

A few days later they met at a canoe club dinner in New York, but neither claw-hammer coat nor white tie could smother the fire within them as they discussed the merits of their respective boats.

"The Chrysalids don't ziz-zag when they're paddled, as the keelless Red Lakers do," observed the Vice.

"Nor do they keep within hailing distance in a breeze in which even a dead log would run and be joyful," retorted the Commodore.

"They need no lee-board to keep them from drifting down the wind," said the Purser.

"Nor more than three men to land them on a shore upon which a gentle tug at the painter will beach a Red Laker," said the Cook.

"Give me a boat," said the Vice, "which steers in the ordinary ship-shape manner."

"I," remarked the Commodore, "prefer one whose

Commander don't have to analyze a whole rope yard before he can get her into sailing condition."

"The idea of oil-cloth decks for any sort of a craft!" exclaimed the Purser.

"Or of decks that make you imagine it's resurrection morn, and you're crossing the Styx in your own coffin," said the Cook.

"Order, gentlemen," shouted the ruler of the feast; "if you've any personal difficulties to settle, please retire to the ante-room, and cease disturbing the club."

"Ze ante-room," remarked the caterer, "is full of ze Alderman an' ze Judge, who fight about ze merits of ze Rob Roy boats an' ze paper canoe."

"Then I will settle the question myself," said the President, taking from his pocket a copper cent of the fathers. "Heads signifies the superiority of the Chrysalids, tails of the Red Lakers."

The coin spun in the air, and the quartette sprang to its collective feet. It came down exactly edgewise into a bit of Fromage de Brie, and so remained.

APPENDIX.

IN the preceding pages the authors have introduced in a desultory way some hints which it is hoped may prove of practical use to inexperienced or possibly to experienced canoeists. There are some questions however which are asked by every one who contemplates engaging in this delightful recreation, and to a few of these questions answers are now volunteered.

I. Where can I get a canoe?

The best answer is a list of builders. James Everson, Williamsburgh, N. Y., W. Jarvis, Ithaca, N. Y., and George Roahr, Harlem, N. Y., build excellent boats after the Nautilus model and its modifications. These all build on the well known lap-streak or clinker plan, using cedar planks and oak timbers. Mr. J. H. Rushton of Canton, N. Y., builds after the Nautilus and Rob Roy models, also after a model of his own. He has a peculiar method of construction, which makes his work very strong and serviceable. Walters & Sons, of Troy, N. Y., build paper boats after the Nautilus and Rob Roy models, D. Herald, of Rice Lake, Ontario, Canada, builds canoes on a model of his own approximating to the best type of Indian "birch." His method of building is described on page 106. The model is admirable for speed, sea-worthiness and safety. At Ottawa, Canada, is a builder named English whose boats are well spoken of but the authors are not personally acquainted with them. J. F. West, of East Orange, N. J., builds light and serviceable boats of ash strips covered with painted canvas. He does not build for sale, but will furnish information for those who wish to build for themselves.

II. How much does a canoe cost?

Seven dollars a foot is not an unfair rule whereby to estimate the cost of a lap-streak, Nautilus model, including spars and rudder. Some builders charge more, others less than this. The Canadian canoes are cheapest of all, but to the first cost must be added the tariff duty for importation into the United States (about thirty per cent ad valorem). Herald's highest priced canoe, seventeen feet long, was at latest advices forty-five dollars. This size is built under his patent and copper fastened throughout. Built in the rib and-batten style, the price is ten dollars less and canoes of smaller sizes of both kinds still less. The Nautilus models are largely decked over fore and aft without extra cost, and are provided with ample water-tight compartments which are invaluable in case of accident and may be fitted with hatches which render them available for stowage. The other models whose first cost is less, are not provided with these conveniences except by special arrangement, involving of course additional expense. A canoe may be purchased and fully rigged for less than a hundred dollars if her purchaser is gifted with mechanical ingenuity. Or if money is no object, the cost may be run up to almost any figure. The ordinary price of a double-bladed paddle is in the United States five dollars. All the builders make them. A specialist is Henry Mitchell, of Bergen, New Jersey.

III. Miscellaneous.

For sails use the best unbleached heavy twilled cotton sheeting, double width. Cut so that the selvedge will form the leach of the sail. Hem half an inch wide, stitched on both edges. Strong laid cotton cord about an eighth of an inch in diameter should be sewed along the luff of the sail, and is by no means undesirable along the other edges, loops for making fast being provided whenever needed. All these cotton articles should be well soaked before being made up to prevent unequal shrinkage. The plates entitled " Under full sail," and " Close hauled " give a sufficiently accurate idea of the size and shape of sails. The " Chrysalid," as drawn, is supposed to be fourteen feet long, and the " Red Laker" seventeen feet. From this the size of the sails can be easily ascertained. The flying jib shown in one of the cuts is of no practical use, and no one is advised to rig one.

Laid or braided cotton cord of one-eighth-inch or a little more in diameter is best for running rigging. For painter use braided sash cord, or best Manilla hemp.

Probably the best varnish for canoes, spars, paddles, etc., is " Pellucidite " Nos. 1 and 2, made by Seely and Stevens, of No. 32 Burling Slip, New York. The same house has " paste filling " which should be applied before the varnish. The best brown shellac is very good and possesses the inestimable virtue of drying in ten minutes. It may be applied over the paste filling above mentioned. All varnishes are better and clearer for being laid on and suffered to dry in the sun.

All metal work about a canoe should be brass or copper. If it is nickel-plated, so much the better.

Decks or coverings of some sort are essential. These

may be fixed as in the Nautilus model, or movable, which is better for obvious reasons. Canvas, rubber, or glazed cloth serve very well. A simple and inexpensive device is to sew small rings in the edges and hook them over small round-headed brass screws set along the gunwale. Let the screws be either on top of the gunwale or under it. If set along the outer edge they are sure to be knocked off. The authors, after a trial of flexible covers, have decided in favor of wooden decks, fastened along the gunwale with simple keys, staples, or buttons. If cloth is used ridge-poles are necessary to make a watershed. Wooden decks should be cambered or arched for the same reason. The open central space should have a flexible cover available in rain.

Some of the open canoes have thwarts which are curved downward. This makes them uncomfortable to sleep in, and the builder should be directed to curve them upward. They can be easily changed if desired.

The masts should be stepped in fixed copper tubes, because these relieve the canoeist from the often difficult task of feeling about blindly for the lower step in the bottom of the boat, and because an accidental starting of the mast may lift it clear of the step, in which case, lacking the tube, it will inevitably split the deck. Suitable tapered tubes known as hose-pipes are kept in stock by dealers in copper tubing. The taper is an advantage as the mast cannot well be stuck fast therein. Cost only a few cents.

Bags of cork-shavings, air-pillows, tin cans, or other like devices may serve open canoes instead of the watertight compartments of Nautili.

Melted candle grease rubbed into a crack will make it

temporarily water tight. White lead is more permanent, and gutta-percha softened in warm water and pressed in is highly recommended. This last is not vouched for personally.

Fine copper wire is very useful about a canoe for lashings, etc:

Very light and easily working mast-rings may be made by stringing wooden or glass beads on stout copper wire, which is then bent to the desired size. Solid rings without beads (or " pearls " in strictly nautical phrase) are apt sometimes to hang on the mast. The beads serve as little wheels in running the sail up and down.

The " latteen " rig is very pretty, but very dangerous. It is not recommended. The " standing lug " which is, in effect the latteen with nearly all the dangerous part cut off, works very well.

A lee-board may be used to advantage in working to windward. It should be hung over the lee-side a little forward of amidships. The simplest way of making it fast is to pass a line through holes in its upper edge so that turns can be taken over the cleats used for sheets. The strain of a lee-board is quite heavy and all its connections must be made strong. It has of course to be shifted from side to side as often as the canoe goes about.

In paddling some sort of a cushion or elastic seat is necessary. Abrasions and possibly more serious difficulties will follow a disregard of this advice.

Do not undertake to be a canoeist unless you can swim easily and well, and do not attempt to sail until you are well accustomed to your boat under paddle.

To render cloth of any kind water-proof the following recipe may be found useful:

Into a bucket of soft water put half a pound of sugar of lead and half a pound of powdered alum: stir at intervals during a day or two until a clear, saturated solution is formed. Pour off into another vessel, soak the cloth therein for twenty-four hours and then hang it to dry in the shade without wringing. By this process an insoluble salt is deposited on the cloth fibres and the fabric will shed water like a duck's back. Woolens such as good Scotch tweed, retain their water-proof qualities indefinitely, cottons not so long.

A glue which is practically water-proof may be made by boiling isinglass (Russian is best) in skimmed milk. The proper proportion is about two ounces to a pint. Common glue treated in like manner is rendered a good deal more capable of resisting moisture than when made with water in the usual way.

THE END.

PUBLICATIONS OF G. P. PUTNAM'S SONS.

*FOR LIBRARIES, TEACHERS, STUDENTS, AND FAMILY USE.
COMPREHENSIVE, COMPACT AND CONVENIENT
FOR REFERENCE.*

THE HOME ENCYCLOPÆDIA

OF BIOGRAPHY, HISTORY, LITERATURE, CHRONOLOGY AND ESSENTIAL FACTS.

COMPRISED IN TWO PARTS.

Price in Cloth, $9.50; in half Morocco, $14.50.
SOLD SEPARATELY OR TOGETHER.

PART I

THE WORLD'S PROGRESS

A Dictionary of Dates, being a Chronological and Alphabetical Record of all Essential facts in the Progress of Society, from the beginning of History to August, 1877. With Chronological Tables, Biographical Index, and a Chart of History,

By G. P. PUTNAM, A.M.

Revised and continued by F. B. PERKINS. In one handsome octavo volume of 1,000 pages, cloth extra, $4.50; half morocco, $7.00.

CONTENTS:

THE WORLD'S PROGRESS, 1867—1877.
THE SAME 1851—1867.
THE SAME FROM THE BEGINNING OF HISTORY TO 1851.
UNITED STATES TREASURY STATISTICS.
LITERARY CHRONOLOGY, ARRANGED IN TABLES: HEBREW, GREEK, LATIN AND ITALIAN, BRITISH, GERMAN, FRENCH, SPANISH AND PORTUGUESE, DUTCH, SWEDISH, DANISH, POLISH, RUSSIAN,
ARABIAN, PERSIAN AND TURKISH,
AMERICAN.
HEATHEN DEITIES AND HEROES AND HEROINES OF ANTIQUITY.
TABULAR VIEWS OF UNIVERSAL HISTORY.
BIOGRAPHICAL INDEX, GENERAL.
THE SAME OF ARTISTS.
SCHOOLS OF PAINTING IN CHRONOLOGICAL TABLES.

"A more convenient labor-saving machine than this excellent compilation can scarcely be found in any language."—*N. Y. Tribune.*

"The largest amount of information in the smallest possible compass."—*Buffalo Courier.*

"The best manual of the kind in the English language."—*Boston Courier.*

"Well-nigh indispensable to a very large portion of the community."—*N.Y. Courier & Enquirer.*

PART II

THE CYCLOPÆDIA OF BIOGRAPHY

A RECORD OF THE LIVES OF EMINENT MEN

By PARKE GODWIN.

New edition, revised and continued to August, 1877. Octavo, containing 1200 pages, cloth, $5.00; half morocco, $7.50.

The Publishers claim for this work that it presents an admirable combination of compactness and comprehensiveness. The previous editions have recommended themselves to the public favor, as well for the fulness of their lists of essential names, as for the accuracy of the material given. The present edition will, it is believed, be found still more satisfactory as to these points, and possesses for American readers the special advantage over similar English works, in the full proportion of space given to eminent American names.

FROTHINGHAM (OCTAVIUS BROOKS) **The Life of Gerrit Smith.** With portrait on Steel, and other illustrations. Octavo, cloth extra, (*In Press.*) . . . .

The life of one who was an earnest philanthropist, a devoted worker in the anti-slavery cause, and a clear-headed man of business, who had an active and important part to play in the history and development of his native State, and in the reform movements of the whole country. The volume is of moderate compass, and presents in an artistic narrative the story of a life of unique character and value.

MAZADE (CHARLES de) **The Life of Count Cavour.** Translated by GEO. MEREDITH. Octavo, cloth extra, . . $3 00

The life of Cavour is the record of the founding of the Kingdom of Italy, or rather of the forming of the Italian Nation. The biographer has brought to this work a hearty appreciation of and admiration for his subject, a full knowledge of the history of the time, and a terse, epigrammatic style; and the translation has been performed with taste and accuracy. The volume is alike indispensable to the student of modern history, and fascinating to the general reader.

PROCTOR (RICHARD A.) **The Myths and Marvels of Astronomy.** Octavo, cloth. $4 00

Mr. Proctor is always an interesting writer, and has taken for his present work a subject that under the dullest treatment would be fascinating reading. A large part of the volume is devoted to the Science of Astrology, which has itself produced a library of literature, and in the remaining chapters he discusses the long list of legends and marvels which the imagination of man has from time immemorial associated with the heavenly bodies.

SELECT BRITISH ESSAYISTS (The) A series planned to consist of half a dozen volumes, comprising the representative papers of *The Spectator, Tatler, Guardian, Rambler, Lounger, Mirror, Looker-On*, etc., etc. Edited, with Introduction and Biographical Sketches of the Authors, by JOHN HABBERTON.

Vol. I. THE SPECTATOR. By ADDISON and STEELE. Square. 16mo, cloth extra, ... $1 25

Vol, II.—SIR ROGER DE COVERLY PAPERS. From *The Spectator*. One volume, square, 16mo, cloth extra, ... $1 00

Vol. III.—THE TATLER. . . . .

"Mr. Habberton has given us a truly readable and delightful selection."—*Liberal Christian.*

"The series will doubtless tend to revive a more general interest in a class of works which, in spite of the standard character conceded to them, are now greatly neglected."—*N. Y. Tribune.*

VAN LAUN. The History of French Literature. By HENRI VAN LAUN, Translator of Taine's "History of English Literature," the Works of Molière, etc.

Vol. I.—FROM ITS ORIGIN TO THE RENAISSANCE. 8vo, cloth extra, $2 50.—Vol. II.—FROM THE RENAISSANCE TO THE CLOSE OF THE REIGN OF LOUIS XIV. 8vo, cloth extra, $2 50.—Vol. III.—FROM THE REIGN OF LOUIS XIV TO THAT OF NAPOLEON III. 8vo, cloth extra, $2 50.

The Set, three volumes, in box, half calf, $13 50, cloth extra, $7 50

"Mr. Van Laun has not given us a mere critical study of the works he considers, but has done his best to bring their authors, their way of life, and the ways of those around them, before us in a living likeness."—*London Daily News*

Lightning Source UK Ltd.
Milton Keynes UK
UKHW030310230620
365391UK00013BA/3154